WHO'S YOUR DADDY?

Second edition

A Guide to Genealogy from Start to Finish

All forms in this book may be downloaded free at:
www.WhosYourDaddyBook.com

WHO'S YOUR DADDY?

Second edition

REVISED, UPDATED, LARGER PRINT

A Guide to Genealogy from Start to Finish

Carolyn B. Leonard

All forms in this book may be downloaded at:
www.WhosYourDaddyBook.com
Copyright © 2018 by Carolyn B. Leonard

No part of this publication may be reproduced, stored in a retrieval system, or transmitted in any form or by any means, electronic, mechanical, recording or otherwise, without written permission, except in the case of brief quotations embodied in critical articles and reviews. Although the author and publisher have exhaustively researched all sources to ensure the accuracy and completeness of the information contained in this book, we assume no responsibility for errors, inaccuracies, omissions, or any other inconsistency herein. Some names have been changed to protect their privacy. Any slights against people or organizations are unintentional.

Who's your Daddy? *(2nd Edition)*
A Guide to Genealogy from Start to Finish
ISBN 13: 978-1-883852-08-5 (softcover) 10: 1-883852-08-0
Daddy 13: 978-1-883852-11-5 (e-book) 10: 1-883852-11-0
Hardback ISBN 978-1-883852-19-1
All rights reserved, First edition 2009, Second edition 2018.
Library of Congress Control Number: 2018906060

Rev 45678910
Visit the author's web site: www.carolynbleonard.com

Manufactured in the United States of America
Buffalo Industries, LLC
OKC 73162

*Figure 1: Genealogy is like a box of chocolates.
You never know what you are going to find
when you open the box.
If you can't get rid of the skeleton in your
closet, then you must teach it to dance.*

DEDICATION:

Ernest S. Branch (1905-1969), a born scribe and family historian. He taught us to be proud of who we are and where we came from, no matter how limited we might be in material possessions. He saved our family history with his story-telling talents.

And to Jon—my proofreader, roommate, fellow searcher, husband, *mi amor*, and friend.

With thanks to all those fellow writers, friends, family, librarians and encouragers who have helped me and shared their stories, as well as all the friendly people we met on this journey.

A special thanks to map graphics designer Judith Mills, artist Linda Matheson, comma queen Rosemary Hardage, editor Marcia Preston, and first publisher Dan Case, without whose help this little book would never have seen the light.

PREFACE

Who's Your Daddy? is a basic guide for the "rest of us," those who are more interested in learning about their heritage than about creating a philosophical tome.

Who's Your Daddy? encourages you to have fun with your new hobby while reminding you to follow the rules of recording sources so you don't wind up with egg on your face.

Who's Your Daddy? shows you how to research at home, on the Internet, in county court houses, in libraries, in cemeteries, in church records, and—best of all, on the road to visit the places where your ancestors lived, loved, and died. (Note: Genealogy provides a great excuse to travel!)

Who's Your Daddy? explores basic rules of genealogical evidence, evaluation of source materials, research methods, and includes extensive guidance on web-based research and DNA study. Plenty of "True Story" examples and clear illustrations are included to show you the way.

Who's Your Daddy? covers *WHY* you should do the work, HOW you can research and write the stories, *WHEN* it is time to stop and publish your book.

This revised edition reflects new and updated websites, improved strategies for locating records, the latest software programs for recording your findings, and suggestions on getting your memoir or family history saved and in print. The address of Internet pages referred to is included, as well as many new illustrations and photos to improve your experience.

Index to True Story Examples:

Chapter	Subject	Page #
2	**Les and the Dress**	**14**
3	**Alpha and the Strippers**	**23**
	The family puzzle	21
	The Twins go to war	22
	Interview agreement	28
	Miller's Law, John & Abigail	31
4	**Grandmother and the census taker**	**37**
	German immigrants	39
	Kidnapped by Indians	40
6	**Tryphena's 1779 birth certificate**	**81**
8	**Surprise cousins from Minnesota**	**91**
	An 8-year-old query answer	96
10	**William the Conqueror**	**100**
	Solomon becomes Slamon	103
11	**Six tombstone inscriptions**	**106**
	Finding Uncle Levi	107
	Geocaching	112
	Finding early family cemeteries	115
	Five tiny stones	122
12	**The weeping Angel**	**132**
	Alexander's LAST wife	133
	First murder	134
13	**The "Jones" family museum**	**149**
14	**A birthday cake on the copy machine**	**156**
	Illinois courthouse disaster	159
	Elizabeth's children & guardianship	167
	A burned county	175
	Elusive marriage records	178
15	**Travel for genealogy**	**189**
	Visiting a college library	190
16	**The long, hard journey**	**193**
	A moving target –county lines	196
17	**Confederate claims**	**204**
	Pension file info	207
	The 7 sons of Abraham Dudrey	209
18	**DNA and Knighthood in England**	**220**

.... Joan Case finds her Indian   222
19 ....Chronology for Cornelius   **225**
20 ....Publishing your book   **237**

Table of Contents

1) Why Do It and Where to Start...1

2) Who Do You Think You Are?... 13

3) Interviewing Grandma.. 19

4) Taking the Census, an Overview... 35

5) That Beautiful Old Handwriting 51

6) Dating Old Photographs 57

7) Recording Sources... 75

8) Getting Organized.. 85

9) Posting Queries 91

10) Spelling Doesn't Count 99

11) Tiptoe through the tombstones......................................105

12) Gardens of Art..125

13) Genealogy Programs 145

14) Courthouse Treasures 153

15) Books and Libraries...181

16) Maps and Migration Patterns 191

17) Was Great-Grandpa a Soldier?..197

18) What about DNA...215

19) The Dating (and Calendar) Game...................................223

20) Getting it in print 231

CHAPTER ONE

Why Do It and Where to Start

Finding your Family's Place in History

Doing the paperwork and citing your sources is a lot of work and paper shuffling. Some people call genealogy "an unending term paper," and in a way it is. However, for a hobby that revolves around dead people it is amazing how much fun you can have.

Here are Ten Good Reasons to Start.
- ✓ You want a fun, rewarding hobby. Genealogy is one of the top three hobbies in the nation, along with gardening and coin collecting. Just ask any librarian; they will tell you their genealogy sections are always busy.
- ✓ You want to confirm or deny those family stories of famous/infamous family members.
- ✓ You want to understand how all those cousins are actually related to you and to each other.
- ✓ You have a passion for history—and that passion will become more intense as you learn your family connection to historic events.
- ✓ You need to compile your family medical history because of congenital health problems.
- ✓ You have a desire to join one of the many hereditary societies such as Daughters of American Revolution (DAR) or Sons of American Revolution (SAR), Daughters or Sons of Union or Confederate Veterans, etc.

- ✓ You want an excuse to travel.
- ✓ You want to help your children find their family's place in history.
- ✓ You come closer to understanding yourself by learning about your ancestors and their lives.
- ✓ Admit it—you enjoy the hunt for your roots!

Let's Begin—But How?

As the saying goes, "The longest journey begins with a single step." Just begin with what you already know. The most useful information will be your own knowledge of yourself and your family.

Start small—with yourself.

Two forms are essential to keep you on track.

1) The Ancestor Chart (AC).
2) The Family Group Sheet (FGS).

These two forms are available free online. Go to *www.whosyourdaddybook.com* and select the form you wish to print.

I designed these simple forms (Ancestor Chart and Family Group Sheet) especially for beginning family historians. Librarians tell me the commercial forms are confusing, but the public loves mine. I hope you will too. Examples are below. You will need several copies of the Family Group Sheets. Print these out and fill them in with a pencil.

Simple Ancestor or Pedigree Chart (AC).

Sometimes called a pedigree chart, the AC provides the roadmap for your genealogy search. These charts provide an overview of your family, making it easier to track your research progress. This chart will help you discover what you know and do not know. Personal knowledge can form the first limbs of your family tree but do it in pencil until you have the proof.

Fill in the AC with a pencil, beginning with yourself. You will probably need to research to fill in the blanks for birth, marriage, and death dates. Begin with the records you have at home.

Just as you filled in the information about yourself, now enter the information on the ancestor chart for your mom and dad, your grandparents and great grandparents and so on, including as much data as you can find. These charts help you connect the dots in the right order and will serve as a roadmap to keep you on the right path.

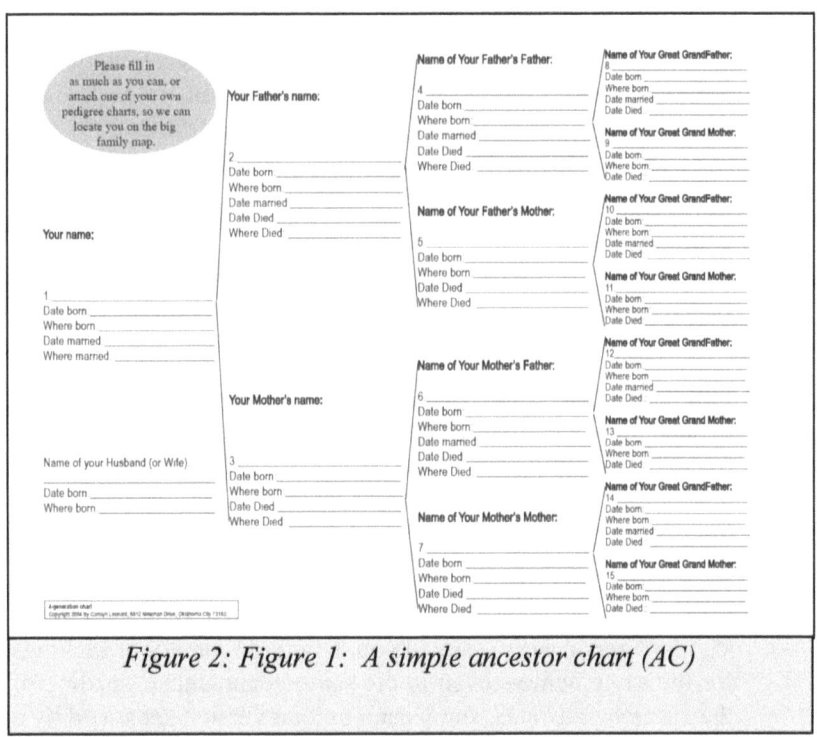

Figure 2: Figure 1: A simple ancestor chart (AC)

What Is the Least You Need to Know to Begin?

- ✓ You need to know the complete name, the dates and places of birth and marriage for yourself, your parents, and your grandparents. Begin searching for birth, marriage, and death certificates, obituaries and other documents that might provide names, dates, and locations to prove the data you have already entered. Look at your family Bible records, old letters, and family memorabilia. Clues may be found on the backs of old photographs. Gather everything you have—papers, photos, documents and family heirlooms. Rummage through your attic or basement, filing cabinet, closet ... wherever you may have stashed old papers and family records.

You may be surprised at how much information you already have. Don't be overwhelmed by the amount of historical information you have to hunt for.

How to Fill in the Forms:

- ✓ Use a pencil: Ancestor charts and family group sheets should be written in pencil until you have documentation for each entry. (Note: Pencils are usually the only writing instruments allowed in research facilities.)

- ✓ Enter your name on line one. If you are a married female, enter your full maiden name. You may notice on the ancestor chart that all the even-numbered entries are for the males in your family and uneven numbers go to females. This will be important later.

- ✓ Full names: Fill in the rest of the names as best you can. Be sure to use full names and maiden names for females. In earlier records the wife may have been referred to only by her husband's name. (Example: (Mrs. John SMITH). In such cases, use parentheses to show her name is not yet known.

- ✓ Surnames: Print the SURNAME in all capital letters. The given name (first & middle names) is never all caps. Spelling was not standardized in early years so you may find a variety of spellings for the same name—even in the same document. If spelling of the surname changes, show each unique version separated by a slash; e.g., Cozine/Cosine/Cosyn/Kosijn.

- ✓ Nicknames: Use birth names and add nicknames in quotes.

- ✓ Dates: Record dates in military style: day - month - year, using three letters for the month and all four numerals for the year, for clarity and readability, e.g., 21 Aug 1957. Sometimes the exact date may be unknown. In those instances, use a qualifier or a common abbreviation such as: about/abt/@, or more commonly, ca for circa, after/aft, before/bef, estimate/est. Note: with these abbreviations no period is used.

- ✓ Counties: Include the county in place names. Counties are very important because you usually find the sources and proof for your data in county record archives. Also show town, township, state, and country. If you are unsure of the location but have good reason to believe it is a certain place, use probably or the abbreviation prob preceding the name of the place.

County Names are Important.

If you only know the city and state of an event, the National Association of Counties has a website (www.naco.org) to help you find the name of a county. At that website just enter the zip code or name of the town to bring up the county name. You can also find cities within a county within a state the same way. To reach this website, type into your computer search engine the words "find a county." That will bring up a list of places to look. Google is one example of a search engine.

From the resulting list of choices, try "National Association of Counties" or from the main website www.naco.org, choose from the top menu "about counties," pull down to "Data & Demographics" and then click on "City Search."

Here are some examples of places to look:
- ✓ Family Records—Bible record, family history, traditions, stories, county history books, old letters, photos.
- ✓ Scrapbooks—Baby books, wedding books, albums, funeral books, autograph albums.
- ✓ Newspapers—Clippings of obituaries or anniversary stories.
- ✓ Family Heirlooms—Quilts, engraved jewelry, locks of hair, samplers, old diaries, jewelry from patriotic and fraternal organizations.
- ✓ Legal Papers—Wills, deeds, land grants & patents, mortgages, voter registration forms, military papers, passports, school records, health records, citizenship papers.
- ✓ Miscellaneous—Journals, announcements, evidence of memberships in social and professional organizations.
- ✓ Old Photographs—Information on family photographs, front and back.

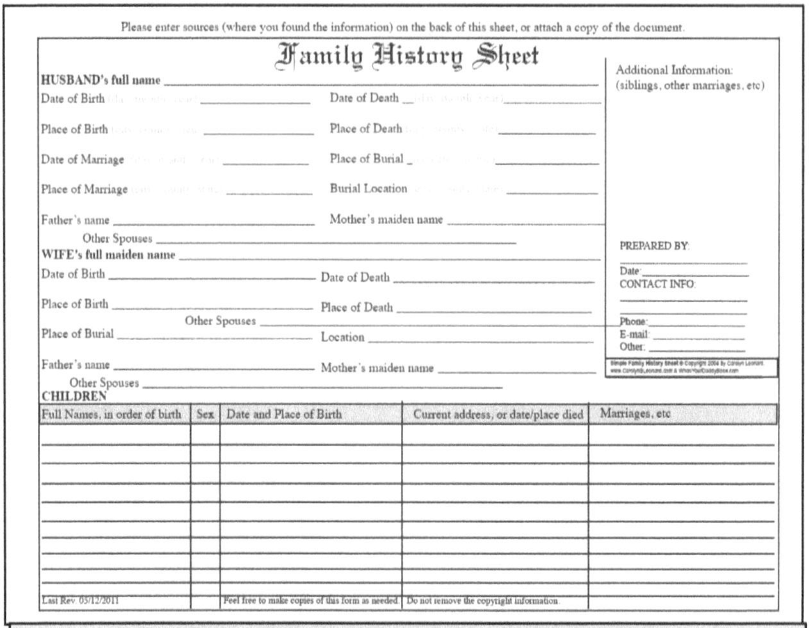

Please enter sources (where you found the information) on the back of this sheet, or attach a copy of the document.

Family History Sheet

HUSBAND's full name
Date of Birth — Date of Death
Place of Birth — Place of Death
Date of Marriage — Place of Burial
Place of Marriage — Burial Location
Father's name — Mother's maiden name
Other Spouses
WIFE's full maiden name
Date of Birth — Date of Death
Place of Birth — Place of Death
Other Spouses
Place of Burial — Location
Father's name — Mother's maiden name
Other Spouses

Additional Information: (siblings, other marriages, etc)

PREPARED BY:
Date:
CONTACT INFO:
Phone:
E-mail:
Other:

CHILDREN

Full Names, in order of birth	Sex	Date and Place of Birth	Current address, or date/place died	Marriages, etc
Last Rev. 05/12/2011		Feel free to make copies of this form as needed	Do not remove the copyright information	

Figure 3: A simple Family Group Sheet (FGS).

A Simple Family Group Sheet (FGS)

Go to www.WhosYourDaddyBook.com to print out the forms. Fill out a separate family group sheet for each family union—one for you and your children, one for each sibling and their children. If there are children from a second or third marriage, fill out a different FGS for that union.

Next, do an FGS for your grandparents, both maternal and paternal, including their siblings (your aunts and uncles) as the children. Aha! You are catching on quickly.

Just enter the relationships by blood. Later, we will show how to include collateral relationships and marital relationships. Eventually, you can add stepfather, half-brothers, third cousins twice removed, and so on. Simply enter names, places and dates of birth. When applicable, add date of death. You will be surprised how many dates and places you may not remember, and this will provide a ready reference. I even use it to remember family birthdays.

Can You Find That Again?

Finding a Family Register from a Bible like the one shown is a rare stroke of luck. Be sure to include documentation for each piece of information, right from the beginning—where did you find the information? Where could a stranger find that same information? Enter the source for each item, on the back of the FGS sheet. Later, when you are working with a computer program, you will add this source in the reference section.

Often, Bible records are the only source for births, marriages, and deaths. Family Bible records are one of the most coveted sources for family researchers. If found, they may add multiple generations to a family tree and explain how family members are related to each other.

Be sure to keep lots of notes on the forms explaining where each piece of information came from. Examples: Family Bible in possession of (name & address); Great-Aunt Mary's recollection on (date); etc. No matter how much basic information you collect, none of it will be accepted by a lineage society without a primary or secondary document proof.

Those little pieces of paper prove we lived—birth certificate, marriage bond, death certificate or any other vital source. Items recorded close to the time of the event are best. Note in your source record full contact information for the person or organization that has the item in their possession.

The goal is to have source citations that will enable anyone to find and verify each statement on the family group record, or to allow you to go back later to recheck the information as recorded. If you don't document the information at the time, it is almost impossible to find the source again later.

Why take time to record where you found the information?

For items such as a marriage license or death certificate, it is good also to make a photocopy to keep with the Family Group Sheet. Then file the original in a safe place.

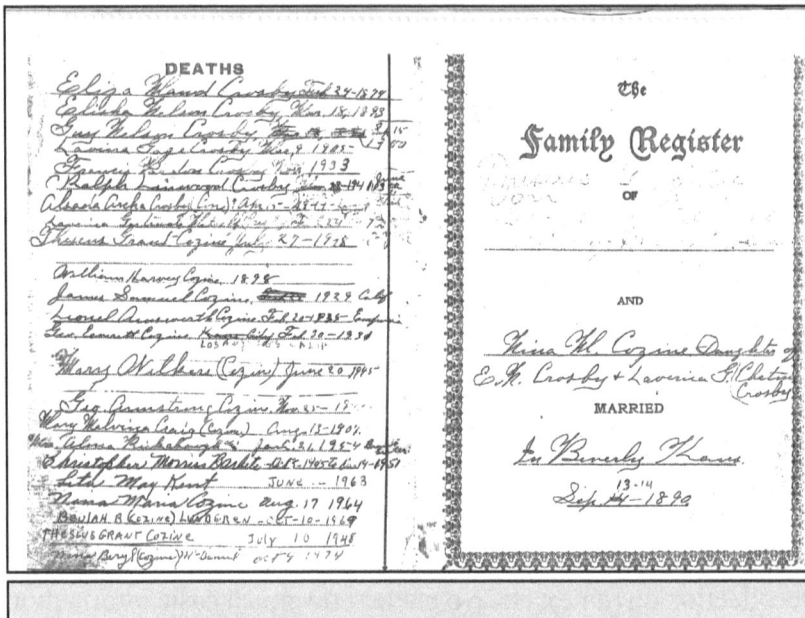

Figure 4: Nina Crosley Cozine's Family Bible.

Using a pencil, get started entering data now so you can see how easy it is to do. Fill in what you can. Don't worry if you don't have all the facts. Chasing missing links is the fun part of the treasure hunt.

Why Do We Want to Know all This?

Learning about your family's place in history makes all history come alive for you. No matter how bored you were in your U.S. History class in high school, your whole outlook changes once you learn you had a patriot ancestor.

The search is not about collecting names. It is about connecting with your ancestors lives and developing the personalities of the past. Focusing your family history search helps keep your research on track, and also lessens the chance of overlooking important details when you have too much information coming in too fast.

When you have entered all the data on hand, check with your relatives to see if they can fill in any of the remaining blanks with information you did not know. Ask if they have any family documents they are willing to share with you in return for copies of your compiled data.

Keep in mind that sometimes people are afraid to admit they have a Bible record or other keepsake fearing you will want to take it. Assure them you only need a copy of the document. They can keep the original.

And Then, What?

Later you will enter all your information into a computer program that will help you keep it organized. You can print out the completed sheets to share. Handwritten forms work best in the beginning while you are locating source records, and even later when you are on the road. You may find conflicting data. You will need to track down original records to determine which is correct.

Why Do I Have to Use a Pencil?

Use a pencil because you will probably make mistakes in the beginning. When you talk to older family members, they may give you conflicting information. You will have to research to learn the facts. Pencils have handy erasers.

I did genealogy work by hand for many years. Later a typewriter seemed wonderful. Now I use the computer with a genealogy program and wonder how I ever kept track of all those handwritten notes and dates.

Start with yourself and work back in time. Always try to gather as much information as possible on each generation before moving to the next-earlier generation. Do not expect to find someone who has already gathered all your family information and is just waiting for you to ask. Most historians have invested years and considerable expense in their research, and they guard that information jealously, for good reason. For instance, to ask for *"everything you have on John Smith"* will not be well received. You must let them see you are worthy of receiving information.

Clues to your family history may be found scribbled on photographs. You might find names, dates and places on the back. Be sure to note the name and address of the photographer, usually shown at the base of studio card photographs. This may give a location where you might learn more about their lives. The style of dress may help identify the time period of the photograph.

Ancestor Charts, Like Little Twigs, Grow up

Maternal ancestors are those on the mother's side of the Ancestor Chart. Paternal ancestors are on the father's side—the surname you received at birth. Both are your direct, or lineal, ancestors.

Collateral relationships are found between individuals when neither person is directly descended from the other. Brothers, sisters, aunts, uncles, nieces, nephews, and cousins have a common ancestor, but they are not your direct lineal line. These collateral lines are important, however, and can often lead you to finding a lost ancestor when you hit a brick wall in your research.

I suggest you pick just one family surname and focus on that at first. Otherwise you may become overwhelmed.

If you trace your family tree down from a single ancestor, it is known as a descendant tree.

If you trace the family back through generations from a single individual, you have created an ancestor tree.

Not counting second marriages, an individual will usually have two parents, four grandparents, eight great-grandparents, sixteen great-great-grandparents and so on.

Always start with the known and work on the tree from the known to the unknown.

Family Questionnaire

When preparing to interview a distant relative, fill out a Family Group Sheet including as much detail as you can. With this partially completed FGS in hand you will be able to ask for the exact information you need.

In Summary:
- ✓ Finding out who you are and where your family fits in history is important to each of us.
- ✓ Knowing our heritage gives us a sense of responsibility and self-esteem.
- ✓ Begin with yourself.
- ✓ Using proper forms keeps you on track.
- ✓ Identify sources from the beginning

CHAPTER TWO

Who Do You Think You Are?

Writing a Memoir

Before you move to interviewing others, you may want to write your own story. This will help you know what to listen for with your relatives. Tell your story plainly and with directness; write truthfully, remembering that a touch of humor makes for easier reading. Your goal is to put your information in a form interesting to other family members.

Is It Worth the Effort?

Never underestimate the effect your written words may have on unborn generations in helping them through the storms of life. They may appreciate your life story as a precious treasure and bless you all their days.

Many years ago, my father learned he had terminal cancer. He was the last of his family as far as we knew at that time. I bought him a tape recorder and asked him to record his memories. He followed up by telling some great family history stories with details we would not have known. He talked about growing up in horse and buggy days and his amazement at living to see men walk on the moon. He told his hopes for the future successes of his grandchildren. He even sang a couple of the songs I remembered him singing to me in childhood, like *Redwing,* and *Standing on the Promises.* That was more than thirty years ago, yet my brother and I still treasure that tape, now transferred to recordable disc, as do my children and their cousins.

What Is a Memoir?

A memoir is a piece of autobiographical writing, usually shorter in nature than a comprehensive autobiography or family history.

The memoir, especially as it is being used in publishing today, usually tries to capture certain highlights or meaningful moments in one's past, often including a contemplation of the meaning of that event at the time of writing the memoir. Rather than documenting every facet of a person's life, a memoir may be more emotional and focus on capturing particular scenes or a series of events.

Begin by brainstorming on paper all your life events that were either very positive, or important in a negative way. Select the one event that seems most interesting to you to write about first. Good memoirs are about common everyday things in life. These events can be interesting, sometimes just as interesting to read as a good novel and may be helpful to others encountering the same situation in their own lives. A memoir is expected to be true, so be careful not to exaggerate or embellish the truth.

Following is an example of a brief memoir that reveals how experiences in elementary school, painful at the moment, can influence our thoughts years later.

TRUE STORY: Les and I had not seen each other for years, but recently we reminisced about our fifth-grade school play when I recited "*Frost is on the Pumpkin*" and he was the Mighty Wongaloo, singing "*A Happy Wanderer.*" Les had a good voice, but in practice one day his voice cracked. I giggled. He blushed. The teacher scolded me. I didn't understand what I had done wrong. Later, my mom explained how a boy's voice would change at that age. However, Les confessed he never sang in public again after that.

Moreover, Les recalled getting in trouble for calling me a bad name that year. I remembered those details very differently—he made fun of my new dress, and I never wore it again. That incident remained a painful memory to me, and it was still hard to discuss at our reunion twenty-five years later. Recently I finally put the events in perspective.

The rest of the story? I kind of liked Les then, and I probably initiated the misunderstanding by asking if he liked my dress.

This was no ordinary dress. It was my first "store-bought" item and it came from a new dress shop named *Nita's Toggery*, on main street of our small town. I thought it was the most beautiful dress in the world. Mom was a good seamstress and stitched my clothing just fine, even if they were from printed feed sacks. But that dress was special! I remember it well. A pale lavender and mint green plaid bodice with a full circle lavender skirt and one of those little bolero tops just coming into style. I begged and begged until Mom finally bought that dress for me.

Les said the dress made me look fat—actually what he said was the dress made me look pregnant. He laughed. At age eleven I was so insulted I went home crying, tore off the dress and threw it on the floor. I think my mom called the principal, so Les got in trouble and had to apologize to me the next day. The apology didn't matter. I refused to ever put that expensive dress on again, and Les was off my best-friend list forever.

This week I pulled that painful memory out of my past and pushed it into the sunshine so I could look it over. What was I expecting a twelve-year-old boy to say? *"Oh yes, that is a lovely dress."* Really?

All I remembered were my feelings of humiliation. I never considered Les' feelings. I had no idea that my fifth-grade giggle may have forfeited a young boy's possible career in music. Today we can empathize with the children we were at the time and laugh about the experience.

Writing Your Own History

Here are some thought starters for writing your own story:

Begin with yourself: Tell when and where you were born, along with any stories you've been told surrounding the event. Do you know about your family surname? Country of origin? Did the spelling change when your ancestor immigrated?

Tell about your childhood: Fun activities shared with your siblings, visits to grandparents, relatives you remember, financial condition of parents, and religion in the home. What stories have come down to you about your parents or grandparents or other distant ancestors? Are they reluctant to talk about their past?

Is there a mystery? Are any secrets hiding in your family history you wish you knew more about?

Your brothers and sisters: Name, date and place of birth, accomplishments, names of spouses, date and place of marriage, occupation, education, their children. Are there any traditional names in your family? Any famous—or infamous—relatives? Have the stories grown in retelling?

Describe your school days: Schools attended, favorite teachers, achievements, humorous situations, was there a bully in your school? How did you react? Who or what influenced you to take certain courses or do certain things you might not have done?

Explain your activities: Vacations, jobs, church activities, sports, tasks at home, fun and funny situations.

Talk about courtship and marriage: Where and how you met your spouse, special dates, how the proposal was made, the wedding, parties and receptions, honeymoon, what influenced you in your choice of spouse.

Describe your married life: First home, starting housekeeping, spats and adjustments, financial challenges, joys and sorrows. How did your parents and grandparents meet and marry? Are there family secrets of lost love, jilted brides, arranged marriages, elopements, unusual courtships?

Detail your vocation: Training for your job, promotions, companies worked for, salaries, achievements, and awards. Historically, how has your family supported the family? Are they farmers, engineers, or doctors?

Your children: Names, dates and places of birth, health, characteristics, growing up, schooling, marriage, vocations, accidents, accomplishments.

Civic and political interests: Positions held, services rendered, clubs, fraternities and lodges you joined and why. Have any historical events affected your family? How did they survive the Depression? Did conflict over some national event (Civil War, Vietnam, etc.) cause a break in family relationships? Any stories about a great fortune lost or almost made? Are such incidents laughed about or regretted?

Detail your church activities: When you became active and why, churches attended, offices held, answers to prayers, your belief system.

Your avocations: Sports, hobbies, drama or music, reading interests, travels, favorite songs, movies, books, writers, poems, etc. Have any old family recipes been preserved?

Celebrations or holidays you remember: Birthdays, Easter, Christmas, special vacations. How are holidays celebrated in your family now? How in the past? Which ones are most important?

Your plans and hopes for the future: What about family reunions? How often? What happens there? Any traditional foods, customs, and activities? Are records kept? By whom? What expressions are used in your family?

Your ancestors: Impressions of those you knew, knowledge of those you did not know but learned about. Do you have a favorite ancestor? What impressed you about them? Is there a family cemetery? Any family heirlooms that have been handed down? Who is the family scribe? Who has the family photos?

Your encouragement and counsel to your descendants: Tell what you have learned that is of lasting importance, perhaps an obligation to your country, church and family; suggestions about honesty, humility, health, diligence, perseverance, thrift, loyalty, kindness, reverence; your religious beliefs, and your hope for the future? This would be the takeaway.

This exercise in writing your own story will be of great help as you begin encouraging others to record their experiences.

In Summary:
- ✓ Writing your own life story will help prepare you for interviewing others.
- ✓ A memoir is a piece of writing about one's life, usually considerably shorter than a full autobiography.
- ✓ The memoir captures certain highlights or meaningful moments in one's past.
- ✓ Explaining how you responded to certain experiences in your life may be helpful to others.

CHAPTER THREE

Interviewing Grandma

Who you gonna ask and what you gonna ask 'em?

     Lucky me! When I was growing up, my dad was a born storyteller. On cold winter nights after the chores were done and supper was over—we never ate "dinner" in those days—we would gather around the fire in the living room and beg Dad to tell us a story. I would climb up on his lap, until I got too big to do that, he'd pull out his old guitar and sing some cowboy songs.

    TRUE STORY: He told us stories told by his dad, Alpha Branch, who died of cancer long before I was born. Alpha had been orphaned as a lad and his uncles raised him.

    When Alpha turned 21, the minimum age for homesteading, he registered to run for land in the new state of Oklahoma. His older brother, Will, joined him in the plan. Alpha bought a little black range pony and trained it for the race while Will prepared a team and wagon to carry the supplies and camping equipment they would need. Alpha and Will lined up with other contestants at the state line near Anthony, KS, and waited for the soldiers guarding the line to fire the gunshot that would signal the opening. Alpha knew there would not be enough quarter sections of land for everyone, but he was going to give it his best.

When the race began, Alpha and Will became separated in the dust and confusion of thousands of hopefuls on every kind of contraption imaginable – including one man on a tall three-wheeler bicycle.

Alpha did find an unclaimed quarter and staked his claim. But he was alone on the prairie with no food or drink. He couldn't go to look for his brother because he had to stay to defend his claim from claim jumpers. Night came, so he removed the saddle and tied Little Black's reins to the saddlehorn. Then he lay down next to the pony and took a nap. In the middle of that dark night, one of those noisy prairie thunderstorms hit, frightening the horse, who ran away.

Figure 5: The Samuel C. Branch family about 1875.

In later years, Alpha said the next morning a cold, wet, and hungry but wiser young man gathered sticks to start a fire and contemplate his grim situation. He said It was almost noon before he dried off and stopped shaking in the damp air.

And then, his brother pulled up with the supply wagon and he knew together they would be all right.

In another story, Dad would often remind us of a puzzle—his father Alpha had a brother named William and a sister named Mabel who were only cousins to each other. How could that be? Dad would say that was the family mystery and it was our job to solve it.

Eventually we did solve the puzzle, and the resolution piqued my interest in genealogy.

Dad's grandfather Samuel C. Branch had been married to Ann and had a son named William. Ann died in childbirth at age 26.

Samuel then married Caroline, age 19, and they had a son, Alpha, my grandfather.

Samuel died age 39, and his young widow Caroline married Samuel's twin Stephen. They had a daughter named Mabel.

William and Alpha had the same father; Alpha and Mabel had the same mother. All three had the same last name, Branch.

So, William and Mabel did not have a common parent and they were cousins because their fathers were brothers. They did each share one common parent with Alpha, their half-brother.

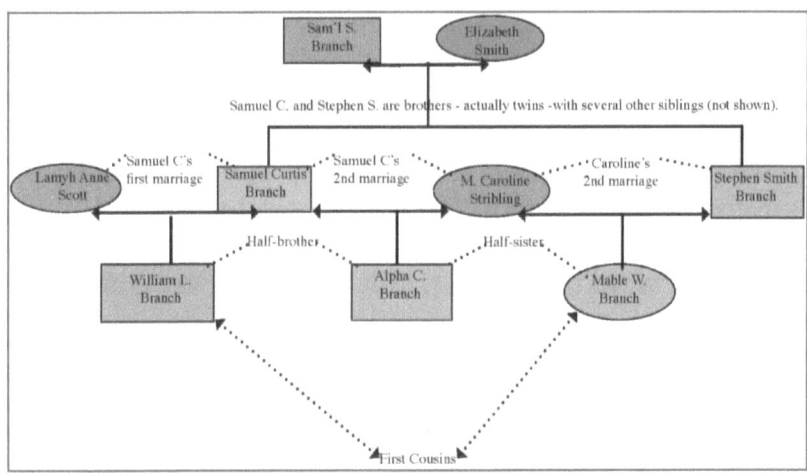

Figure 6: Family Mystery Relationship solved.

A family illness took their young siblings

Mystery solved. Alpha really did have a brother named William and a sister named Mabel who were only cousins to each other. Samuel and Caroline had three other children who died young, probably of "lung disease" or TB. Mortality was high among children and infants at that time.

Here is an interesting tidbit in regard to the 1875 family photo: Samuel is already dead at age 39 and the photographer just painted in a picture of him with his family, using an earlier Cabinet Card photo.

Caroline at age 28 in the photo is actually a widow with three children. The baby, Viola, and the young girl, Arvilla, died soon after. Caroline only lived to age 38.

Back then, there was no cure for consumption, now known as tuberculosis (TB). Whole families, like this one, would be afflicted with the wasting away disease as it spread through the air from one to another. But the medical profession didn't know that yet.

How did I learn all this? Research!

The twins march off to war.

TRUE STORY: Samuel Branch and his twin brother Stephen Branch went off to the Civil War. They served four years in the same outfit, as privates in Company G of 62nd Illinois Volunteers, and stayed together through the war.

Wealthy people had the option to hire a "substitute" to fight in their place—the going rate by 1863-64 was $300. The Branches were not wealthy, but they were landowners so the boys probably could have found a way to stay home with their families.

Obviously, the Branch twins, Samuel and Stephen, either could not or would not do this.

This information came from their military records and Stephen's pension record. The pensions were not authorized by the government until several years after the war. Samuel didn't live long enough to get a pension. Soon after returning from the war, Samuel died. Five years later Caroline married his twin, Stephen Branch. While the twins, Samuel and Stephen, remained close knit in life, they and their wives were widely separated in death.

We found Samuel's grave in Illinois, Caroline's in Missouri, and Stephen's in Oklahoma. Wonderful stories—of course none of them were written down until long after all the people who could have answered questions about them were gone.

Figure 9: Sam'l C. Branch (1835-1875)

Figure 9: Caroline Stribling Branch (1847-1885)

Figure 9: Stephen S. Branch (1835-1911)

But at least the family mystery was solved, and the puzzle became part of our family legend. Are there any family mysteries or legends in your family? While you are collecting family records, also set aside some time to interview your relatives. Try to collect stories, not just names and dates, and always ask open-ended questions so you don't get just a "yes" or "no" without any details. There is always at least one family member who carries the stories inside his brain.

Find the family history keeper

Interviews may make you nervous, but this is probably the most important step in researching your family. Don't put off visiting Uncle Jack or Great Aunt Martha until it is too late.

Be prepared. You will not find perfect people. Our ancestors made mistakes. They had weaknesses and strengths. They were human then, just as we are now. Some people may be hesitant to tell the whole story. You may hear many versions of the same story since each person's point of view is different, and everyone remembers an event in his or her own unique way. Those differences are what make the compiled history so interesting.

Practice, Practice, Practice

Practice on yourself. Ask yourself the same questions you plan to ask others and write down the answers. Then go to your older relatives, asking them for their help in saving the family folklore. Each interview quickly leads to another: *"You should talk to Uncle Phillip about that."* As you continue your search you will find relatives you didn't even know about.

Take a Recorder and Camera

A notebook and some pencils will get you started, but you may get so interested in the story you forget to write anything down. Back at your computer, you can't remember exactly what was said. Tape recording the interview is good. Doing both, recording and taking notes, is better. Your recording may be quite lengthy, and the notes should help you find the exact information you need from the tape.

Contact the person you'd like to know better and set a mutually convenient time. Explain what you want to know and why, so they will have time to think about it and remember or find the information you want. You might ask an older relative to look through a family trunk or attic with you. The objects may jog their memories. Allow plenty of time. Let them know your schedule, one hour at the most. You don't want to wear them out. Share what you have already learned. Ask if they have some old family memorabilia but assure them you only want to photograph the item. You promise not to damage it in any way. Their old family records, letters, and souvenirs may help you expand your search.

Interview Introduction

Begin with an introduction to remind you of important facts about the recording.

Here is a suggestion:

"This is an interview with _____, [present/ former/ retired title] _____, who now lives in [city & state] _____.

[Then give a one-sentence biographical sketch containing information relevant to the topic of the interview: e.g. Mrs. Smith will be giving some of her memories about her grandparents, John and Mary Brown.]

This interview is being conducted on [date] _____, at [place of interview]_____. The interviewer is [Give your full name] _____."

You should record this introduction on the tape before starting the interview, then rewind and play it back to check the equipment and the sound quality.

Practice at home so you are comfortable with whatever equipment you plan to use. Bring along extension cords, extra batteries and tapes. Before you start the interview, be sure to eliminate all unnecessary background noise. Once you've tested your recorder, you can relax and enjoy the revelation.

Your subject may feel uncomfortable at first with the machine running, but it is quickly forgotten. Your job is to help them relax and forget they are being recorded. Good to tell the person being interviewed they do not have to answer if a question bothers them.

Make your initial visits short, especially with someone you are just getting to know. Be cautious about inviting additional people. Occasionally a guest may help the narrator to feel at ease, but even a spouse can cause interruptions and confusion. Better to let the story flow uninterrupted and make corrections later.

A simple camera is another good piece of equipment to bring along. Use your camera to record the setting and also to copy photos or other materials.

I recommend completing two forms before going to your interview: one is a Family Group Sheet (FGS) with information relevant to the subject. The FGS, completed with as much information as possible, gives you a roadmap so you can follow what the person is telling you and who they are talking about when they say, *"Uncle Fred/Joe/John said..."*

The other form you need to complete ahead of time is a release (see sample following), which should be signed by the person you are interviewing, so you both are clear on what information can be shared and under what conditions you plan to use what they tell you. I usually agree to furnish them a rough draft of the transcript. This allows them to make minor corrections, deletions, and additions so that the transcript accurately reflects not only what was said, but also what was intended.

Stick to your promised schedule; watch for fatigue. Your job is to let your subject talk and do not interrupt.

Interview Tips—A Personal Visit

Here's a list of "ifs" and a few "don'ts":

Perhaps you traveled a long distance to visit relatives, so you may want to get all the information on one visit. But proceed gently. If Grandma is reluctant to give details, let it go for now.

If your subject is hesitant for you to use a recorder, explain you want to be sure you get the information right. Promise that you won't betray his/her trust and keep your word. You want to be able to listen closely to what they say and not be distracted by taking a lot of notes. If the person agrees to the recorder, keep the tape running. Don't cause distraction by turning it off and on. Often the best quotes happen when you think the interview is over.

If possible, place the tape recorder in a place where the person can't watch it. Most people will talk more openly if they are not focusing on the fact they are being recorded. If you hear a name or place you are not familiar with, jot a note to ask them later how to spell it. Use one- or two- word notes to jog your memory later about other questions you may want to ask. Most people get nervous when they see an interviewer taking notes, so before the interview tell them you will be making notes for this purpose. Try to listen for a meaning behind the stories you hear. Sometimes what you are hearing is more about a family value than about the tale itself.

Writing Down the Bones.

I like to use regular spiral notebooks for taking notes whenever possible, using only one side of the paper. I also use highlighters and a red pen to mark what seems especially important so I can find it easily later. It is better to have too much information rather than not enough, especially because you may not have the opportunity to interview this person again. Once a notebook fills up and I have extracted the data needed for the family history, I enter the date on the cover and file the notebook.

Be sure to number your pages, no matter how rapidly you write. On the first page, enter the name of the person you are interviewing and the date of the interview. This will be invaluable to you later.

This documentation may be needed when you or your great-grandchildren want to use your project. It is extremely hard to go back later and try to document your source.

All along the way, collect and organize photos to illustrate your findings. That helps put flesh on the bones.

What If They Don't Want to Talk?

Most relatives you contact will be delighted at your interest in family history. A few may be uncooperative and even hostile, worrying that you may learn and reveal too many family secrets. Some family members may be concerned about the intimate nature of information or fear you may shake a skeleton out of the closet. To get around that, promise to let your informants see what you have written before it is too late to alter the manuscript. If the person says, *"I don't want to talk about that,"* do not push. Be patient. The "shameful" information may be only a divorce or a long-standing disagreement with another family member. The full story will eventually come out. If it really is something scandalous, you can read about it on newspaper microfilms on your own time.

Interview Agreement

I (the interviewee), _____, hereby give permission to (interviewer) _____ to publish, duplicate, or otherwise use and dispose of the recording and/or transcribed interview recorded on (date) _____ and any videotaped footage and still photographs taken during the interview.

This includes the rights of publication in print and in electronic form, such as placement on the Internet/Web and in other electronic formats, and permission to transfer the interview to future technological mediums.

I interviewee), _____, hereby give the interviewer the right to a copy of the recording and a typed transcription for posterity to family members, libraries and/or educational institutions for scholarly and educational uses and purposes.

I (the interviewer), _____, hereby agree to preserve the products of this oral history interview and agree to provide the interviewee with access to the taped interview, if desired.

Note any restrictions:
Interviewee's Signature:_____
Date _____
Narrator's Address: _____
Narrator's phone number (___) _____
Narrator's email:_____
Interviewer's Signature_____

Interview Question Examples.

Prepare a list of open-ended questions you want to ask, or get your subject started with a story you have heard in the past.

This is probably the most important step in researching your family. You want more than simple one-word answers; you want feelings, stories, and descriptions from their memories to put some flesh on the family bones. Use the questions as a guide, but let your relatives go off on a tangent if they wish. You may learn important things you had not anticipated hearing and would not have thought to ask.

Don't be afraid of silences and don't rush your subject. Be ready with a new question or thought when the well of conversation begins to go dry. In fact, you may want to give your subject the list of questions beforehand to help prime the pump.

Ask your questions with a personal focus. For instance, I wish I had asked my mother-in-law, "How did you, a young woman fresh off the farm in Illinois, meet and marry a graduate of George Washington University in the nation's capital?" Bringing along an envelope of old photos or documents is a helpful tool also. Once you get them started, keep your mouth shut. Interviewers often try to interrupt to get specifics, but it is better to let your subjects tell what they want to tell. Don't rush them and do not be afraid of silences.

Forty Questions plus a few extra.

Here are suggestions to help get the interview started (or restarted):
1. What is your full name?
2. When and where were you born?
3. What are your parents' names? Where were they born?
4. Can you describe the house where you grew up?
5. How did your family come to live here/there?
6. Did your family call you by a nickname?
7. What are the names of your brothers & sisters?
8. Do you know their birthdates?
9. What kind of games did you play?
10. What was your favorite thing to do for fun?

11. Did you have family chores?
12. What was your least favorite?
13. Did you have a job outside the home?
14. Where did you go to school? Did you attend college?
15. In what school activities & sports did you participate?
16. Did you have any pets?
17. What kind of pets and what were their names?
18. Was your family active in a church?
19. Did you have a best friend growing up?
20. Where were you when any war ended?
21. How would you describe a typical family dinner?
22. What were your favorite foods?
23. How were holidays celebrated in your family?
24. Did your family have any special traditions or sayings?
25. What do you know about your family surname?
26. Is there a naming tradition in your family?
27. What legends about family have come down to you?
28. Are there any stories about well-known relatives?
29. Any physical characteristics that run in your family?
30. Are there any special heirlooms, photos, Bibles?
31. What is/was the full name of your spouse?
32. When and how did you meet your spouse?
33. What did you do on dates?
34. Where and when did you marry?
35. What memory stands out most from your wedding?
36. How would you describe your spouse?
37. What do you admire most about your spouse?
38. What is the key to a successful marriage?
39. How did you find out you were going to be a parent?
40. How did you pick out your children's names?
41. What was your proudest moment as a parent?
42. What did your family enjoy doing together?
43. How did you choose your profession?
44. What most valuable thing did you learn from parents?
45. What have you accomplished that makes you proud?
46. What do you hope people remember about you?

Hold the interview to no more than an hour or two at the most, even if you have come a long way. When the interview is complete, thank your subject for sharing the information and promise to send a transcript for them to keep. Keep that promise.

Your Job is NOT to talk

Your chief task is to listen. It is good to make the person feel relaxed and to guide the interview when needed, but the best interviews are when the narrator does all the talking. Don't interrupt. If you need to ask a question, make it open-ended. Don't ask one that can be answered with a single word.

Follow Miller's Law

Do not believe everything you hear. You may find, as I have, that many things are based on fact, but the whole truth and nothing but the truth is quite different.

There is a principle in psychology called "Miller's Law," and that theory can be summed up in a statement made by George Miller, a Princeton Professor and respected psychologist.

"In order to understand what another person is saying, you must assume that it is true, and try to imagine what it could be true of."

Most people apply Miller's Law in reverse. They assume what the other person is saying couldn't possibly be true, and then they try to imagine why they would say anything so ridiculous. Most of the time, we don't really pay attention to what other people are telling us. We want our own turn to talk. We want the other people to listen to us. We want them to hurry up and get to the point. That will not work well here.

Listen to family stories at every opportunity and take notes. Do not argue with your subject even if you know what they are telling you is not correct. They may be sharing subtle information about family mores or politics rather than straight facts.

You will always hear conflicting stories from different sources, and your job is to verify every piece of information—so you can follow Miller's Law and determine what the story is *true of.*

TRUE STORY: I was often told that my great-grandmother Elizabeth Smith Branch was a close relative to Abigail Smith Adams and that grandmother Elizabeth had attended the inauguration of John Quincy Adams. That story was passed down for generations, but after uncounted hours of research in moldy volumes and numerous letters to Adams family authorities, I determined the story apparently holds not a thread of truth other than both Abigail Smith Adams and my great-great-grandmother Elizabeth Smith Branch had the same maiden name of "Smith." Still, the legend refuses to die and turns up in unexpected places. Perhaps someday we will learn how that fairytale started, and what the story is really "true of."

Figure 10: John & Abigail Adams— apparently NOT my cousins after all.

Untangling the family tree limbs.

Change your subject's words as little as possible in the transcript. Type contractions as spoken but leave out crutch words like "you know" or "and-uh" or "and then." Accurately represent the speaker's words, conversational quality, speech patterns, and colloquialisms.

Who, What, Where, When, and Why

Remember the five Ws and an H—who, what, where, when, why, and sometimes how. Try to get all names, nicknames as well as birth names. Some people refer to their first names as their Christian names. The custom originated as the name given at infant baptism in medieval Christendom.

For instance, the Bahr family was Catholic in Germany in the early 1900s. They had seven sons and four daughters. The first (Christian) name of each son was John, and the first name of each daughter was Mary, although they were known by their second (middle) names.

Sometimes only one name or only initials appear on census records so having a choice of names will help identify the subject when you get to that step.

To identify the relationship between any two people, first identify the common ancestor of the two people. A cousin "removed" indicates that the two persons selected are not of the same generation. The chart may be extended in either direction to identify more distant relationships.

In Summary

Items to take along for the interview:
- ✓ tape recorder,
- ✓ microphone,
- ✓ several good-quality 60-minute audio-cassette tapes,
- ✓ extension cord,
- ✓ three-prong adaptor "cheater plug,"
- ✓ two sets of batteries,
- ✓ digital camera,
- ✓ pen & pencils,
- ✓ paper, AC (Ancestor Chart), FGS (Family Group Sheet),
- ✓ release form to be signed,
- ✓ topics to discuss if the well goes dry.

CHAPTER FOUR

Taking the Census, an Overview

What can we learn from those musty microfilm rolls?

After your interviews, a good place to begin is by searching the census records and finding your family there. You will want to see a copy of every U.S. census in which your ancestor appears. It provides a snapshot of the family structure at one precise moment in time.

"Enumeration shall be made within three years after the first meeting of the Congress of the United States, and within every subsequent term of ten years, in such manner as they shall by law direct." (Article 1, Section 2, the Constitution)

Since 1790, the population is enumerated every ten years and the results are used to allocate Congressional seats, electoral votes, and governmental program funding. Some states also conduct additional statewide censuses as the need arises.

Do not be surprised to find across the census years, a wide variation of ages, names, and birthplaces given by the citizens. Evidently "fibbing" about your age is not a new fad, because my great-grandmother never aged in a normal way, according to the census records. Her age changed very little each ten years.

The 1790 through 1840 censuses list names only for the head of household and only the age range of others living there. From 1850 on, you learn the name and age of each person in the household. Additional information is added at each ten-year census.

After 1880 the birthplace (state and country) of the parents is listed with familial relationships. However, census info is not infallible. The ages are often incorrect, and names misspelled.

Keep in mind that perhaps the person who answered the door did not know or had a faulty memory. Once in a while, when the census taker came to the door and nobody was at home, they visited a neighbor and got the family information, which could be very wrong indeed. Remembering we are a nation of immigrants from many different countries, having many different language accents. So, no wonder the census takers had a difficult time getting the names correct. They simply wrote down what they heard.

Cracking the Soundex Code

The powers-that-be created Soundex cards for heads of households for the 1880, 1900, 1910 and 1920 censuses.

In 1935 the National Archives used the Soundex system to index the United States Federal Censuses, beginning with 1880 information, as part of President Franklin D. Roosevelt's New Deal. Hundreds of Works Progress Administration (WPA) workers used this method to provide birth information for the newly-created Social Security System, coding together surnames of the same and similar sounds, but with variant spellings.

Soundexes are arranged by state, with the code of the surname, and given name, bringing together all similar sounding surnames.

The 1880 Soundex cards include only households with children aged ten or younger. Although Soundex is not available for the census years before 1880, those earlier censuses have been indexed and published in books that are available at almost every research facility.

Once you find the indexed entry you will know what microfilm you need to read to learn who lived next door, because often you will find blood relatives nearby.

With computers digitalizing these forms, they are much easier to find and to read.

Figure 11: Census Enumerator with Farmer 1930.

Invaluable Information

Just glancing at the information available on each census reveals the value of these records. That is assuming, of course, you have the right information recorded there.

TRUE STORY: My second great-grandmother Elizabeth (Smith) Branch left us with a mystery on the census of 1880 when she was age 74. All previous information said Elizabeth and both her parents were born in New Jersey. After the death of her husband, we find her (or someone) living in the household of Elizabeth's stepson, Cyrenis "Si" Branch. On the census for his household is listed a Mary E. Branch,

Stepmother, age 74, born in Pennsylvania, and both parents also born in Pennsylvania. If this is great-great-grandmother Elizabeth, all this information is wrong, but we cannot find her listed anywhere else. Nothing matches except the age. The family did live in Pennsylvania a few years before moving to Ohio. Was she confused? Elizabeth has a sister named Mary. Perhaps one of the children relayed the information to the census taker and gave the aunt's name by mistake? We will never know.

What can you learn from Census records?

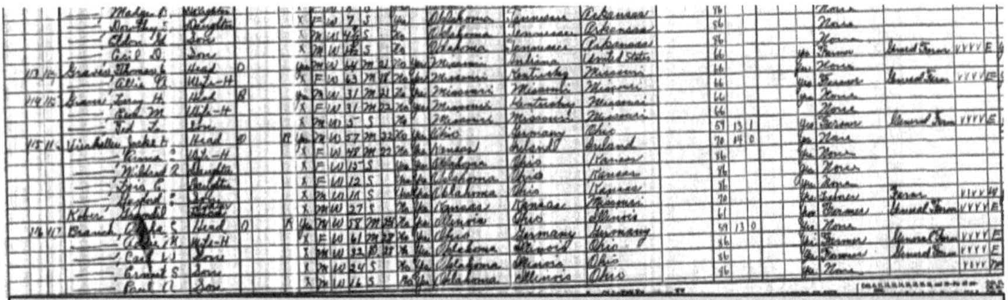

Figure 12: 1930 Census of Little Township.

The 1930 census shows the home address, relationship to the head of household, whether their home is owned or rented, value of home or monthly rental paid, whether they owned a radio set, whether they lived on a farm, their sex, race, age, marital status, age at first marriage, school attendance, literacy, birthplace of the person, and that person's parents.

That's quite a lot to learn from one piece of paper.

If foreign born, you learn what language is spoken in the home, year of immigration, whether naturalized, and ability to speak English. You also learn occupation, industry, and class of worker, whether they were at work the previous working day, and veteran status.

You can sometimes tell that a child was born from a former marriage by following through with the children's ages and birthplace of their parents.

The information you find in the 1930 census includes the name of each person living in that household on the first day of April in 1930, even if they were deceased by the time the census taker came around. Enumerators found the people wherever they were. An earlier image shows a census taker chatting with a farmer at work plowing with horses in 1930.

TRUE STORY: The 1930 census shows the Alpha C. Branch family. Alpha Branch's wife, Addie M. Branch, age 61, was born in Ohio and both her parents were German immigrants. Their three children are listed with their identifying information. Line 46: BRANCH, Alpha C., male, born about 1872, Head of family, dwelling number 116, owned his home, has a radio, lives on a farm, is male, white, age 58. He was 25 years old at his first marriage and he can read and write. He was born in Illinois; his father was born in Ohio and his mother in Illinois. He worked on the previous day before he met the census taker. All this from only one line on the census, and all of this data has proven accurate.

When Did the Census Start?

The first US Census was taken in 1790, but some censuses were taken prior to the Constitution's ratification. Tax and other colonial records exist prior to that date

An early colonial census was taken in Virginia, and people were counted in nearly all of the British colonies that became the United States. You will find a research guide to colonial census records at the Connecticut State Library, which can be accessed on the Internet at this URL: www.cslib.org/colcens.htm or just search for Colonial census.

Why a Census Anyway if not for Genealogy?

The U.S. Constitution requires the government to take a census of the population of the U.S. every ten years. In 1790 we became the first country in the world to call for a regularly held census. George Washington signed the papers making this act a law, and since then a census has been taken in every year ending in zero.

All this information relating to specific individuals is held in confidence for a set number of years from the date of the census, seventy-two years by statute. Therefore, census information is not released as often as genealogists would like. The 1940 census was released in 2012 and the 1950 census will be released in 2025.

One of the main purposes of the census was to provide information on men eligible for the military.

In 1790, we had only recently gained our independence from England, and the men of the day knew it was important to be able to assemble an army quickly if need arose, and of course it did.

Hostilities continued even after the British surrendered in 1781. The Brits continued to harass the American colonies for several years. They also often enlisted the aid of some American Indian nations to annoy and terrify the settlers.

TRUE STORY: In 1790, a group of Pottawatomi kidnapped and scalped one of my relatives in Kentucky. Little Sara Cozine, age 9, remained an Indian captive for five years. They marched her all the way from Kentucky to the British fort at Detroit to collect the five-pound bounty for American prisoners offered by the Brit Commander.

What Happened to the Records?

The British destroyed much of the 1790 Census when they burned Washington, D.C., during the War of 1812. Some state censuses were totally destroyed, others only partially. Some of the early census records were never preserved. Once the data was transcribed and sent to Washington City, the assignment was complete, and the originals were destroyed.

When available, tax lists from the era are used as an alternate source for names to create a substitute for the missing census.

Who's Your Neighbor?

Some records were left in the original chronological order as the census taker visited each household. Others were alphabetized before being copied and turned in.

Where's the 1890 Census?

The 1890 Census was also almost completely destroyed by fire. Some efforts are continuing to resurrect that missing data through tax and other personal records.

For the 1790 census, U.S. marshals (the first census-takers) and their assistants pounded on residents' doors collecting information for nearly seventeen months. The marshals often had to find their way through remote countryside, usually on foot, trying to track down citizens. No matter when the census-taker showed up, the data was supposed to reflect household conditions on the assigned census date, which for 1790 through 1820 was the first Monday in August.

Who Were the Census Takers?

For this first census, the enumerators (marshals or their assistants) used whatever paper they had, ruled it, wrote in headings with pen and ink, then bound the sheets together. It is really amazing that any of the records remain readable. For the 1800, 1810, and 1820 censuses they used schedules of varying sizes and typefaces provided by the state, plus, they had to create two sets of copies of every page.

What Day Was the Baby Born?

Each census year is assigned an official date by the census agency. Enumerators are instructed to ask that answers to their questions be "as of" that official date, no matter when the enumerator may have actually visited a particular household. So, if a baby was born after the assigned census date, and the census taker didn't get around to your house until much later, that baby should not be shown on the census report. The same was true if someone in the household was still alive on assigned date but died before the census taker arrived, then the deceased person should have been counted. Of course, the census takers did not always follow directions well.

To the Bindery and Onward

After the census was finished, the pages were bound into books with two pages facing each other. A page number was stamped on the upper right-hand corner, leaving the other page blank. The pages are now known as A and B pages, with the B page having all the information.

What Can You Learn from the Census?

The information in the next couple of chapters is probably more than you ever wanted to know; however, if you are looking for a particular bit of information, this may save you time in

Figure 13: Writing implements, late 20th Century.

knowing exactly where to look. If you have Native American ancestry, watch for the statement, "Indians not taxed," in certain censuses. They were not included in the census tabulation. Prior to 1870, families of Native Americans who renounced tribal rule and exercised rights of citizens were counted, but others were not included.

With What Did the Census Takers Write

When you complain about difficulty in reading that old handwriting, allow a little sympathy for the writers. Prior to the 1800s, a "pen" generally meant a feather.

Cutting a quill pen required skill learned only after long practice under the guidance of the writing master. One cannot just pick up a goose feather found on the ground wherever you stop and use it as a pen. First, the feather must be drawn or heated uniformly, so as to release the fat from the quill. That process should harden the quill making it suitable for writing. And then it must be sharpened carefully so the quill does not break.

Before Thomas Jefferson died in 1826, his friend Isaac Hawkins traveled to England and studied the pencil industry in the old world. They developed the first mechanical pencil, but the pencils were not in common use until later.

And as for that fading ink you deplore, the material was originally lampblack, gum or soot, a little water, and a binding agent such as animal glue. This mixture was formed into sticks or cakes, dried, and later reconstituted as needed—sometimes thinned too much to leave a permanent imprint. Dark berry juice was sometimes the only ink available.

Sharpened goose quill pens wore out quickly and steel pens replaced them as soon as they became easily available. However, steel nibs did not compete with quill pens until the caustic problems of the ink were solved, as well as refining the metal nib so that it was more flexible and didn't scratch or leave blobs and holes in the paper. There were a few attempts at metal nibs, although feathers were still quite popular well into the 1860s.

In 1861, Eberhard Faber, an American manufacturer, built the first pencil-making factory in the United States, so pencils would have been available by the 1870 census. The Eversharp pencil was a huge success. By 1921 more than twelve million had been sold.

L. E. Waterman received a patent for his "fountain pen" with its reservoir of water-based liquid ink in the 1880s. A great variety of writing utensils gradually became available; however, carved pen staffs and nibs with fancy inkwells remained a standard for elegant writing. In fact, elementary students up through the 1940s and beyond were still using dipping pens and bottled ink for penmanship classes.

The First Printed Census Forms—1830

The 1830 census was the first one where uniform printed schedules were used. The census takers, usually a Marshal on horseback or on foot, brought their blank census sheets ready to be filled with information.

Even with the new printed census forms, their ink was not dependable, their pens dull or sometimes too sharp. Often the liquid ink spread while it dried or dropped blobs on the paper making the information unreadable. Some census takers probably had problems carrying their writing equipment with them on horseback.

Their script may be difficult to decipher, but we should be thankful to have anything readable at all. They had no earthly idea one or two hundred years later people would be pouring over those census records trying to find their family history. The census-taker's assignment was simply to get a head count and certain data required for that particular census year.

In 1830, Congress ordered the 1790 to 1820 records delivered to Washington city. Unfortunately, some of those records never made it to the capitol and remain missing to this day. Officials discovered many of the early censuses had not been preserved as directed.

Figure 14: US Marshals served as the first census-takers.

We Love Xerox!

Now when we need a copy of something, we run to the copier or scan the item into our computer for storage or transmission. However, in earlier years if an office wanted to keep a copy of an incoming or outgoing letter, a clerk had to write out the copy by hand. This technology continued up through 1900.

By 1913 early copying machines were being used. Prior to that, offices employed copyists, scribes, and scriveners—men who typically stood all day or sat on high stools while working at tall slant-top desks.

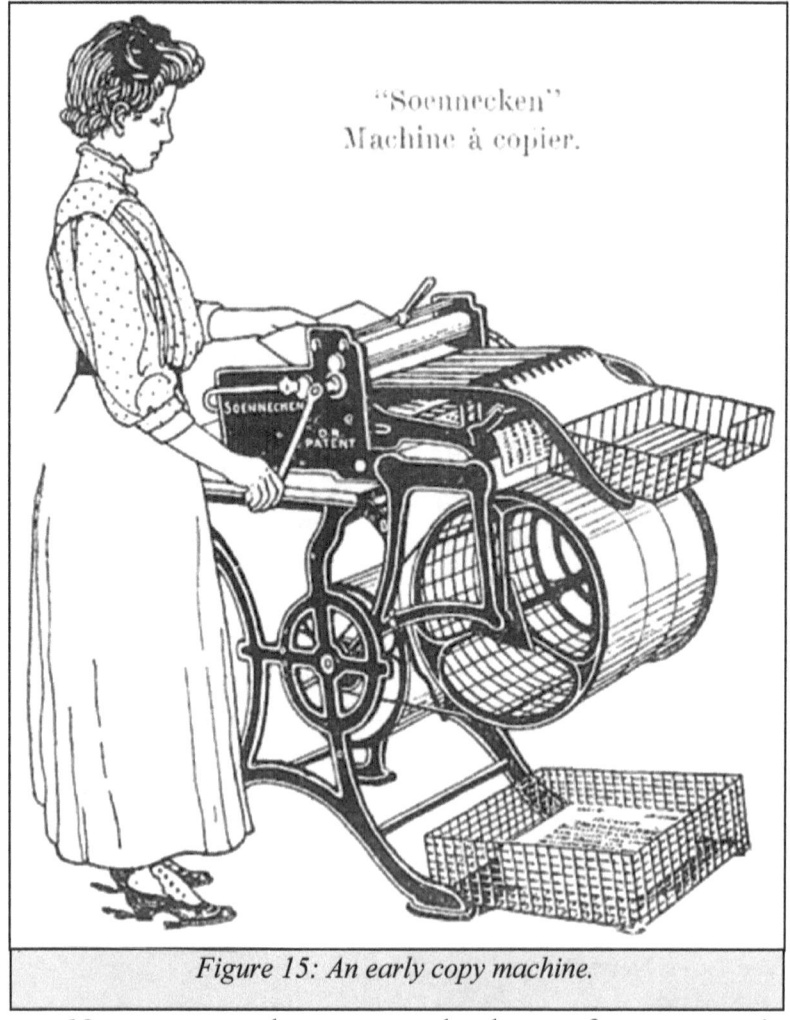

Figure 15: An early copy machine.

Next came carbon paper, the bane of a secretary's existence for the next hundred years. Early carbon paper was messy, did not make a satisfactory copy when the original was written with a pen, and the copies were not admissible in court.

Carbon paper became more important in the 1880s with introduction of typewriters and greaseless carbon paper. Typewriters were able to produce up to ten carbon copies along with an original.

Albert B. Dick invented the Mimeograph stencil, which was marketed by 1890, and that technology remained in use through the 1950s. Models were sold in rectangular wooden boxes containing a hand printing frame with a printing board and a hinged frame that held the stencil. The boxes also contained an ink roller, an inking slate, ink, varnish and a brush for making corrections, waxed stencil paper, blotters, a writing stylus, and a writing plate with a file-like surface.

The Haloid Company coined the name xerography to define the process by which dry ink is placed on paper and began commercial release of its Xerox machines in 1950. Hallelujah! Other companies set themselves up as rivals to the Xerox Company, eventually overtaking their place in the market despite the cultural references to photocopying as "Xeroxing."

Now we lay a paper on the copy machine, push a button and in minutes have as many exact copies as we want.

Who Hired on to Take the Census?

Three people stand between you and your ancestor's data. The person giving the answers, the census taker recording the information, and the person copying the data into the indexes—respondent, enumerator, transcriber. All three people had to be accurate. Your search can be foiled by just one of them making a mistake.

Enumerators after 1880 may have been schoolteachers on summer break or farmers trying to supplement their income. They came from all walks of life. The census takers were required to know how to read and write and they usually lived in the area they enumerated. The government paid the enumerators to go door to door with the goal of getting a head count of all people living in the United States. Then, as today, some were excellent workers, producing accurate, legible records. They took pains to get all pertinent information and enter it on their record papers. Others, however, were mainly interested in payday and did less than an admirable job.

An illustration from Harper's Weekly in 1870 provides insight into what the census taker had to deal with while making his rounds to collect the information.

The census taker could walk many different paths to cover his territory. There was no instruction on the direction he should take, only that he must cover the entire territory assigned to him. People who lived on adjoining property might be listed several pages apart, depending on the route taken by the enumerator. In farm country and early times, the paths of the census takers often meandered in strange patterns.

Figure 16: A census-taker illustration 1870.

1880 Census and Beyond

In 1880, for the first time the Census Bureau hired its own census takers and was given the budget to take full control of the entire census. Federal courts and secretaries of state were no longer involved. The original pages stayed with the county and the first copy went to Washington.

The 20/20 Method of Searching

Sometimes you must use creative methods to find ancestors whose names are missing from the usual census records. When that happens, find them on a previous census and make note of the twenty families before and the twenty after them. Pick an unusual name from that list of forty. The concept is that people moved in packs. They left an area with their neighbors and family branches to start a ready-made community in a new area. So, when you want to find your ancestors on the census before or after that one, scan for the most unusual name such as Rumpelstilskin. More than likely, you will find your "John Smith" living in the same area as Rumpelstilskin on the next census, but your John Smith is listed with a name that has been transcribed incorrectly.

Permission granted to jump ahead

A companion book, "The First Hundred Years" explains in detail what you can expect to learn from each census and what was happening in the country at that time. This information is most helpful for writing family history and understanding what is going on with your ancestors at the time.

For more information and details on the census and events that would have affected your ancestor's lives, check out the companion books, "The First Hundred Years" 1790 to 1890, and "The Second Century."

In Summary

- ✓ Federal census records were taken every ten years from 1790 to the present.
- ✓ The 1930 census asked if the person owned a radio.
- ✓ The census was not planned to be used for genealogy.
- ✓ Most of the 1790 census was burned - by the British in the War of 1812.
- ✓ Some original census listings were alphabetized.

- ✓ The first census takers were US Marshals.
- ✓ Dark berry juice was sometimes used for ink.
- ✓ Before 1913, copies had to be made by hand.
- ✓ If at first you don't succeed, try the 20/20 method.
- ✓ If you cannot find your ancestor where you are searching, perhaps his location was not yet counted in the census. The maps will help you know.

CHAPTER FIVE

That Beautiful Old Handwriting

Working backward.

Because you start your research with yourself and work backward, the first documents you are likely to research are the more recent ones. These are usually not too difficult to read because they are written in a modern hand and modern English, but as you move backward you will find many documents difficult because of terminology and handwriting.

You're Hooked, Now What?

Let's think a minute before diving in headfirst.
Review the information in the previous chapter about the writing instruments of the 1800s.
It may be helpful to enlarge the writing with a copy machine, magnifying glass or your digital camera. As you continue to work with documents you will learn the terminology and recognize the "canned" legal phrases and the important other words important to interpreting the item. In the beginning take time to transcribe every word. Later you will be ready to just do a summary transcription.
Customs change, laws progress, word meanings evolve, occupations become obsolete, and diseases are known by new names. Language is a constantly changing element. Many abbreviations used in early documents are obsolete today.

Making Sense of Scribbles

For instance, in old letters you may see *"In response to your letter of the 21st inst."* The abbreviation stands for "instant," meaning the same month as an already given date. Therefore, if the letter writer has dated his letter August 31, 1883, the 21st inst. is referring to a letter he received in August. If he uses the word or abbreviation "ultimate" or "ult." he would be referring to something that happened the previous month in July.

Trying to decipher handwritten records can cause intense frustration, not to mention brutal eyestrain. Copperplate or English Round Hand, a style of calligraphic writing prevalent in the nineteenth century, is found in use as early as the sixteenth century in Europe. As a result, the term "copperplate" frequently refers to any old-fashioned cursive slanted handwriting. Common problems with reading copperplate include:

- Capital "L" and "S" are notoriously hard to tell apart, especially in unfamiliar names.
- Capital "I" and "J" are virtually identical.
- Double-s may look like "fs" or even "ps".
- One of the most noticeable problems is the letter S. In the handwriting of the period it looks more like an F.
- In some old documents, "th" is written as "y." For example, "Anne Smith ye wife of John died April ye 1st 1654."

The "y" is actually an old Germanic rune called the "thorn" (þ). The Latin alphabet has no letter for "th," so Medieval scholars used the thorn instead, which looks very much like a "y" when written in calligraphy. It was pronounced with the normal "th" sound.

Also remember that spelling and punctuation were not important to early Americans. Words were often written the way they sounded phonetically, and also often by the sound of local accents. Commas, colons, and semicolons drop in haphazardly. A colon (:) may denote an abbreviation. A dash (–) or equal sign (=) can frequently be seen indicating the end of a line or an abbreviation. A double hyphen similar to a modern equal sign

(==) may appear at the end of a line to indicate a word carried to the next line.

It Says What?

Because you always start with yourself and research back in time from there, the first documents you will be working with are more recent ones. These are usually not difficult to read or understand, but as you go further back in time you will find many old wills and deeds that test your patience because of language, spelling, customs and handwriting changes. When transcribing material that is partly unreadable, use blanks for the illegible words.

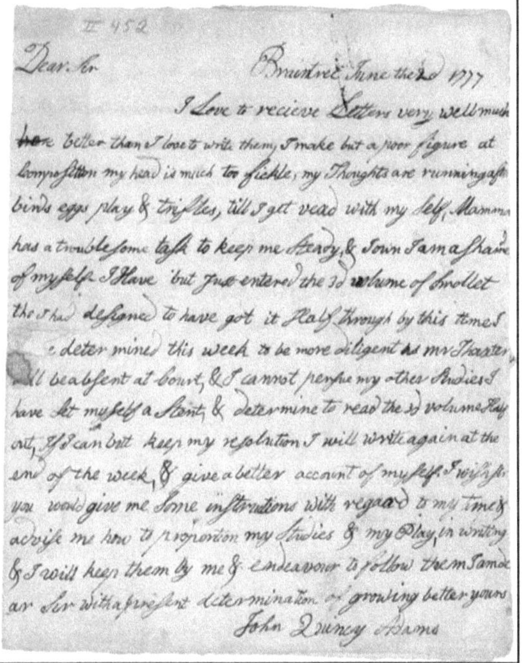

Figure 17: Letter from John Quincy Adams to his father in 1777.

Figure 18: John Quincy Adams as a young man.

Father and son, presidents

John Adams, second president of the United States and his wife Abigail Smith Adams, became parents of John Quincy Adams, who would later serve as the sixth president of the U.S.

Abigail Adams was granddaughter of Col. John Quincy, for whom the city in Massachusetts was named.

Their son, John Quincy Adams, age 10 in 1777, wrote this letter to his father who was then serving in the Continental Congress, and was absent from home for twelve months. The letter is transcribed as young John Q. wrote it, misspelled words and all.

Transcription of John Q. Adams letter (sic)

Braintree June the 2d 1777

Dear Sir

I Love to receive Letters very well much better than I love to write them, I make but a poor figure at Composition my head is much too fickle, my Thoughts are running after birds eggs play & trifles, till I get vexed with my Self. Mamma had a trouble some talk to keep me Steady & I own I am ashamed of my self. I have but just entered the 3d volume of Smollet tho I had designed to have got it Half through by this time. I am determined this week to be more diligent as Mr Thaxter will be absent at Court, & I cannot persue my other Studies. I have Set myself a Stent & determine to rad the 3d volume Half out, If I can but keep my resolution I will write again at the end of the week, & give a better account of myself. I wish for you would give me Some instructions with regard to my time & advise me how to proportion my Studies & my Play, in writing & I will keep them by me & endeavorer to follow them I am de-ar Sir with a present determination of growing better. yours

John Quincy Adams

Old Handwriting is hard to read!

Capital letters are often used to place emphasis on a word such as "Married" or "Died." The first word in a sentence may or may not begin with a capital letter in these old writings. Likewise, words in the middle of a sentence may be unexpectedly capitalized.

Scribes, clerks, and church clergy did not write with the intent that researchers would be able to read their handwriting several years later. In some cases, the writer's objective may have been simply to create an impressive looking document.

Compare while deciphering and match unknown letters, characters, or doubtful words in the same document to determine if they are the same. Compare with words on the same page, and then look on pages before and after the one in question.

Do not spend too much time on one word. Rather, leave the word blank and transcribe the rest of the document, then go back and read it over, using common sense. It should become easier to fill in the missing letters, word, or words.

Court records often use similar legal phrases and standard openings. Wills often begin with the standard phrase, "In the name of God Amen." Probate records may also include standard phraseology, such as "I give and bequeath to my beloved wife," or "my last will and testament." Look for key words in probate records and wills, such as "loving wife," "legacies," or "testament."

Deeds often begin with a set phrase such as "This indenture made and entered into this (date)." Look for key words in deeds and land records such as "appurtenances," "grantee," "grantor." Other early American records may begin, "Know all men by these presents," "To all Christian people to whom these presents shall come, greeting," or they may include this phrase, "In witness whereof I have hereunto set my hand and seal this (date)," or "Signed, sealed, and delivered in the presence of (name)."

Sometimes a stroke, flourish, curl, swirl, squiggle, or loop was used by the writer and may change the appearance of a letter or word. For example, a capital L may look like a capital D. Ascenders or descenders sometimes appear as a curlicue extending above or below the writing line to change the appearance of those letters.

Don't give up! Transcribing documents will help you learn to read the old writing and to understand the terminology.

The further back in time you go, the more difficult the handwriting may become, but as you persevere and grow accustomed to the methods the work becomes easier.

Once you find yourself working in these records, it is always useful to have an aid that you can refer to. An excellent guide with many samples to help you become familiar with the different styles of handwriting is Kip Sperry's *Reading Early American Handwriting*, published by Genealogical Publishing Company, Inc. in 1998. Another resource is *The Handwriting of American Records for a Period of 300 Years* by E. Kay Kirkham, published by Everton Publishers, Inc. 1981.

In Summary

- ✓ Many abbreviations used in early documents are obsolete today.
- ✓ Copperplate often refers to any old-fashioned cursive handwriting.
- ✓ The old-fashioned S often looks more like an F.
- ✓ Other letters are difficult to discern as well.
- ✓ Enlarging the page is helpful.
- ✓ Find a good book on handwriting to help.
- ✓ Reading older documents takes patience and practice.
- ✓ One fundamental practice in reading old handwriting is to compare and match unknown letters, characters, or words in the same document to see if they look the same.

CHAPTER SIX

Dating Old Photographs

Just because an old photograph of your ancestors doesn't have names and dates written on the back doesn't mean you won't find a variety of useful clues for your research. You can often determine the date of a photo from items within the photo that represent a time period such as old cars, household items, clothing, or hairstyles. Be sure to notice the backgrounds and props.

Figure 19: Photographer using a neck brace.

Usually the background is clearly a painted canvas indicating a studio shot. Although painted backdrops were common for decades, the drapes or woodwork, even the stairs may contain clues.

The earliest photo processes were one-of-a-kind, with no way to make reproductions, except by photographing the original image. The gentleman is having his "likeness" made in a photo studio. His head is held firmly in a neck brace to position and prevent movement during the long exposure required.

Daguerreotypes

Figure 20: Daguerreotype of William Dudrey about 1864.

Daguerreotypes are named for the French artist and chemist Louis Daguerre, who first introduced them in the 1840s. The images are negative, but the mirrored surface of the metal plate reflects the image and makes it appear as positive. The images are mirror-like and difficult to see. The best-known image of Edgar Allen Poe was a Daguerreotype.

These mirrored images remained popular until the 1860s. This photo of William Dudrey has the mirror-like effect of a Daguerreotype and is in a case similar to those. The young man was born in 1845 and he appears to be about twenty years old. He probably had his "likeness" made before becoming a soldier in the Civil War. We know from research he joined the 5th Illinois Cavalry when he was 17 years old in 1864.

Ambrotypes

Ambrotypes came next, 1855 to about 1858. The Ambrotype showed a negative image on the back of a glass plate which was then either varnished black or backed with black paper. Although the two are very similar, an Ambrotype does not exhibit the mirror effect of the Daguerreotype.

Daguerreotype and Ambrotype photos were always placed in a metal case, usually with a lid, for protection. These cases displayed a variety of designs. Distinguishing between the two types requires a good deal of skill.

Tintypes Take Over the Market

Tintypes, introduced in 1856, present a negative image on an opaque metal plate. Below, a large tintype is shown beside a usual size tintype for comparison. Before 1865 these tintypes were often placed in Daguerreotype cases, then in cardboard holders. Later they were stand-alone photos. The earliest tintypes are grey-toned; after 1870, they appear in sepia tone. The image might be tiny "gems" as small as one-inch square.

This image of the author's great-grandparents measures about eight inches by ten inches, looks like it was produced on a piece of used roofing tin, with colors added. The large image is not in good condition and is very unusual. Tintypes, introduced in the 1850s, continued to be popular up to the turn of the century. Because we know the child in this photo was born in 1887 and looks to be about five years old, we can date the photo at around 1892.

Figure 21: This 8x10 tintype picture is printed in color on rough tin. The smaller image is the usual size of tintypes.

There are also cabinet card images of these same people in separate images. We know the father pictured in the image died in 1888 when the child was about two years old, so this image was apparently made later, by superimposing the photos on the tin plate.

The tintype and rarer ambrotype have similar and sometimes indistinguishable images. Occasionally the only way to distinguish between them is to look at the back and front of the photo and see if it is made out of glass or iron. The tintype image is flat with a 2-D image. Tintypes are attracted to a magnet, while Ambrotypes and Daguerreotypes are not.

A young Civil War soldier far from home might send his "likeness" home to his mother, family, his wife, or a waiting love.

This soldier pictured is determined to send home his picture no matter how uncomfortable he finds the neck brace to prevent movement. Most likely such a likeness was a CDV or *Carte de Visite*, a descendant of the Victorian calling cards. The CDV photographs are small, sensitized with albumen (egg white). These photos print on thin paper which is mounted on heavier cut cardstock and usually finished about 2.5 by 4-inch size.

Figure 22: Union soldier, sitting in neck brace

"Move A Muscle and I Will Blow Your Brains Out!"

Trying to keep a subject posing for this long process of several minutes must have been quite a feat. The most extreme form of persuasion comes from an article in the *American Journal of Photography*, 1861, where one operator used an unusual method.

"It occurred to him that the strongest of all human motives is fear. As soon as he had completed his adjustments, he suddenly draws a revolver, and leveling it at the sitter's head, he explains in a voice and with a look suggestive of lead and gunpowder: 'Dare to move a muscle and I'll blow your brains out.'"

Cabinet Card Images

Cabinet cards, introduced in 1866, are generally Victorian era family portraits about 4.5 by 7 inches, twice the size of the CDVs.

A paper photograph mounted on thick cardboard, the cabinet cards are durable, and many have survived to the present day. They remained popular from the 1870s into the 1900s. Cabinet cards could be seen across the room when displayed on a cabinet, hence the name. The cards can be further dated by the shape and color of the borders.

Early Photograph Equipment

Photo equipment continued to improve as Edward S. Curtis (1868–1952) recorded the lives of Native Americans across the nation. His cabinet card photographs of the remarkable Yellowstone area influenced U.S. authorities to preserve it as the country's first national park in 1872.

Support the War Effort with Revenue Stamps

As part of the effort to fund the war, several special taxes were levied. One of those was an 1864 act where revenue stamps had to be purchased and affixed to every photograph.

Therefore, any CDV photos with a revenue stamp can be dated in a two-year period between 1 Aug 1864 and 1 Aug 1866.

Figure 23: Revenue Stamps were purchased for photographs in 1864 and affixed on the back of prints.

Traveling Frontier Photographers

By the late 1880s, frontier photographers began traveling throughout the west with large bulky cameras. They used large glass plate negatives that produced excellent images but were messy and hard to handle. Glass plates remained in use among astronomers and other scientists into the second half of the twentieth century due to their superiority for research-quality imaging.

Often, the photographer's covered wagon was his darkroom and he fastened his camera on a tripod. Because of the long exposure time needed, sometimes the people being photographed required a neck brace to keep them from moving, which would blur the photo. Frontier families often wanted their animals in the photo with them, whether work mules, buggy horse, milk cow or dog, and the resulting picture often shows a blur around the animal's tail.

William Prettyman, a frontier photographer in the 1880s used his wagon pulled by oxen to haul his camera equipment so he could photograph the Oklahoma Land Run of 1889. He traveled around and took photos of homesteaders and Native Americans where they lived. Here he is pictured with two yoke of oxen, ready to cross the Cimarron River in Indian Territory.

Figure 24: William Prettyman, frontier photographer. (Photo courtesy of Western History Collections, University of Oklahoma.)

Frontier Photography

Another story is repeated in the *Photographic News* dated 13 August 1886: "There was a lady who visited a frontier photographer in the American West, where there wasn't much but prairie and wind. She said, he arranged me in the chair—an old wooden one—and placed my head in the [neck brace] rest, which was an old pitchfork with the sharp ends broken off. He fixed his camera and then took a huge quid of tobacco out of his mouth, threw it against the wall higher than his head, and said, 'Now look right at that, mum, hold still, and look purty.'"

In early 1900, traveling photographers roamed all over the country taking pictures. They stopped at the frontier homesteads, convinced all the residents to put on their best clothing and come stand in front of their homes to record their situation. Minus flashbulbs, the dark interiors of the dugout or sod homes were rarely if ever pictured, so the pioneer wives pulled out whatever they were most proud of to show in the pictures; a piano, a bird

Figure 25: *A family in their dugout home in the Cherokee Strip about 1894.*

cage, a nice chair, quilts; symbols of their dreams for a lovelier tomorrow.

One family of homesteaders near Woodward in Oklahoma Territory, put on their best clothes and brought out a galvanized washtub along with their good horse and wagon to be in the photo when the traveling photographer came by. The young people are keeping their feet out of the picture. Perhaps they have no shoes. Date of the photo is probably about 1894, soon after the opening of the Cherokee Strip.

The Stylish Ladies Fashions

Women's fashions are the first things to check when trying to date a photograph. Compare them with *Godey's Lady's Book*, now online, which was one of the most popular books of the 19th century. Each issue contained poetry, beautiful engravings, and articles by some of the most well-known authors in America. Old catalogs are also helpful in identifying dress styles.

Prior to 1870 women almost universally wore their hair parted in the center and tied in the back. Bangs became popular around 1910. Men's hairstyles rarely changed, and unkempt beards were reasonably common up to 1900. Books by Halvor Moorshead, *Dating Old Photographs*, and *More Dating Old Photographs*, published by Family Chronicle in 2000, are also good sources to help you with dating old photographs.

Figure 26: Cabinet card photo of the author's 2nd great grandparents, George and Mary Cozine of Emporia, KS, ca.1900.

Study the Photographs

Investigate the photographs and the photographers, kind of like investigative journalism says, "Follow the Money".

For instance, we know that George and Mary Cozine's picture was made between 1885 and 1900 in the studio of L. S. Page, Emporia, Kansas. Research showed that photographer Louis S. Page was born 1843 in Maine, served in the Union army, came to Emporia and established his studio in 1874, according to the website for Lyon County, Kansas. Page was also a Union veteran and may have been a member of the same GAR unit with Cozine. According to Cutler's *History of Kansas*, Page had the leading studio of that area in 1884. George Cozine, a brick mason, was a descendant of Holland Dutch families in Kentucky, as was his wife. Cozine's obituary was published in the *Emporia Gazette* in November 1900, and Page's obituary appeared in 1925.

Figure 27: A rare 1840s Daguerreotype photo, unidentified model.

Figure 28: This lady is dressed in the 1860s Civil War period style in this tintype image.

Bonnets, Bustles, and Babes –

These lovely bonnets and hooped skirt dresses in figure #80, were shown in *Godey's Lady's Book* in 1840.

Notice the lady in the 1860s dress (Figure 79), with her long hair parted in the middle and tied up in a net or snood. She is wearing a fashionable polka dot dress and hoop skirt style of the Civil War period. Having a "likeness" made was quite an event and involved much more than just telling everyone to "smile." Women especially would not have allowed themselves pictured in an out-of-date dress—if they had any to choose from.

Figure 29: Bonnets, bustles, & dress styles from the 1840s.

Figure 30: Mr. and Mrs. Titus Buffington of Xenia, Illinois in a Cabinet Card image.

The back of this studio portrait is labeled Mr. and Mrs. Titus Buffington—but he had three successive wives. Which Mrs.

Buffington is it? I found this 4.2 x 6.5-inch heavy cardstock cabinet card photo for sale on the Internet. The seller noted that on the back of this photo was written, "Grandpa and Grandma, Mr. and Mrs. Buffington."

Using Fashion History to Date Photos

I bought the cabinet card, thinking it could be my second-great-aunt, Hannah Branch, and her second husband, Titus Buffington. It is definitely Titus, but he had three wives. I don't know which one is in the picture.

First, I tried to learn what years Kepley Studio was in business in Xenia, Illinois. No luck there.

The lady is obviously uncomfortable in her tight corset. Although the back is not shown, the dress may have a bustle. Her hairstyle does not tell us much. The two-piece dress and jacket is of a lovely dark brocade with a button-front top and a white lace jabot. She holds a lace handkerchief in her lap. The lower part of the skirt appears to be gored. There are no props visible in the picture. The man is wearing a three-piece suit with a gold chain watch fob and although his hair is still dark, he has a chin-only, medium-length white goatee. We have an 1862 photo of another male with this style of goatee, but we think this picture is from the 1880s.

Studying the Buffington Family History Sheet, I could see Titus Buffington had six children. The first wife gave him five, the second, one child, and the third had none, although I knew some of his grandchildren referred to the third wife as grandma. Titus first married about 1845 to Aleatha Ann Davis when she was 20, Titus 24 but she died in Jan 1868 at age 43 when Titus was 47. The pictured couple appears much older than that, so we eliminate wife number one.

He married second a few months later to, widow Hannah Branch (my relative) in June 1868 when she was 37, and Titus ten years older. The cabinet card, introduced in 1866 remained popular through the 1890s, so at first it seemed possible the photo could have been made before Hannah died in August 1878 at age 47.

Titus's third marriage a year after Hannah's death is listed to the widow Rebecca Fravel Gonterman. She was 51 and Titus 58. They celebrated thirty-three years together before he died at age 90. Rebecca outlived him.

I took the photo to the state photo archivist office for a determination. Much to my disappointment, Rachel Mosman, associate archivist, said the lady cannot be my relative because the dress style with fitted jacket, tight sleeves and gored skirt only became fashionable in the late 1880s. Hannah died more than ten years before the style came into fashion.

The photo has to show wife number three, perhaps it could even be their wedding portrait.

In Summary

- ✓ Study old photographs carefully, recording the name and location of the studio as clues to look for residence information.
- ✓ Lady's dress and hairstyles help date photographs.
- ✓ Daguerreotypes were introduced in the 1840s, followed by Ambrotypes.
- ✓ Tintypes were popular from the 1850s to the 1900s.
- ✓ Small CDV photographs were popular during the Civil War.
- ✓ Revenue Stamps were required for photographs 1864 to 1866.
- ✓ Cabinet Cards remained popular from 1870s into 1900s and many still survive.

CHAPTER SEVEN

Recording Sources

Logging Your Research

It is best to keep a research log on each family so you don't find yourself plowing the same field over and over. Record each and every book, census, etc. and the name of the library where you read any reference material connected to your family. A simple three-ring notebook will work, but I prefer using this research log as a reminder of what information I need to keep and where I found it.

Research Record Log

My name (researcher)____________________
Ancestor's Name ____________________
Date of search ____________________
Where searching (name of Library or other facility) ____________________

Search Date	Document Title & Call No.	Description of item (author/title/year/pages)	Comments/Results (helpful/not)	follow up?

Figure 31: Research Record Log.

Figure 72, Research Record Log, can be downloaded from the website: http://www.whosyourdaddybook.com/

Which Ones to Remember

Primary Sources: Records created at or near the time of an event by a person who had reasonably close knowledge of the event. For example: birth certificates, marriage licenses, census, or letters written at the time of the event. A death certificate is a primary source for date of death, but not for date of birth. Sometimes the old family Bible is the only written record that can be located. Only documents created during that person's lifetime are considered primary.

Secondary sources: Records created a significant amount of time after an event occurred, or by a person who was not present at the event. Examples: military pension record, county history books. Death certificate for date of birth and place of birth are secondary, because the person giving the information may not have been certain.

Record enough information about the source so someone else can retrieve the same information—also so you can go back and verify your own data.

Citation Hints

If you get data from the 1900 census, for example, record the roll number, state, county, city/township, page number, and family number. This way cousin Sue can go look it up easily at her library. An easy way to do this if you are using Ancestry.com, the online genealogy search site, is to copy the information recorded under Ancestry's "Source Citations" on the search page.

Citing a Book Source

For books, record the title, author, publisher, date published or edition, and page number. Note in the margin of the research log from what library, what relative, or what book the information was gleaned. It is best if you can make a copy of the document page showing the item, if possible. This will save much time later if you come up with conflicting data.

Example: Val D. Greenwood, The Researcher's Guide to American Genealogy (Baltimore: Genealogical Publishing Co., 1973), pages 52-54.

I usually also add a note about *where* I found the item, e.g.: *"Saw the book at Oklahoma History Center research library on 1 May 2009."* Sometimes it is hard to find the same source a second time, even in the same library. Include the call numbers for the book as used in that particular library, if you can find them.

Citing a Source

Any statement of fact that is not common knowledge must carry its own individual statement of source. Copy too much material rather than too little and give too much, rather than too little, information on sources. Lineage societies require lots of documentation, and years later some relative may want to use your research.

Do I Need a Form for That?

Sometimes a preprinted form with columns already prepared makes it easier to enter data, like the research log example, but any journal, ledger or notebook will work. Source information should be placed on the Family Group Sheet (FGS) referred to in Chapter One. The log can be downloaded free from the website: http://www.whosyourdaddybook.com/.

Pilgrim's Progress—I Am Born

The federal government does not maintain copies of birth records of persons born in the United States or its territories. Those records would be in the state or territory where the birth occurred−maybe—if it occurred after they started requiring the records to be kept. These records and indexes are stored in a variety of places in each state.

A good book to keep on hand and take along on research trips is *The Handy Book for Genealogists,* published from 1949 to 2002 by Everton Publishers of Salt Lake City. The most recent version available is the 11th edition and published by Genealogical Publishing Company. This version integrates the winning formula of the previous editions with several important new features. The genius of *Handy Book* is its capacity to provide the researcher with at-a-glance genealogical guidance for each county in the U.S. Every chapter begins with an essay about the genealogical history of the state and its records.

What Are Vital Records?

Vital records, called such because they record life's "vital" events, are the growing trunk of a family tree and the most valuable. Records of the births, marriages and deaths of your ancestors will generally be from civil government records back to a certain point in time, which varies by state, parish or country. Prior to that, church or parish registers are the most common source for information. Tombstone records and cemetery records can also provide clues.

Birth certificates, marriage certificates, death certificates, divorce certificates, and adoption records are the best resources to help you as a genealogist. They are available in the state where the event occurred, but each state has different rules and prices for obtaining them. I usually begin entering data from the death record because it is the most current. You can find the Social Security Death Index online free, here: https://search.ancestry.com/search/db.aspx?dbid=3693 or just search for it. Some states even have the complete death certificate or an abstract available for downloading.

Go to the website www.vitalrec.com to learn how and where to obtain these vital records for each state and territory in the United States.

On that web site you can click on the state you want to search. You will find addresses, fees, and web sites for state vital records departments, plus links to free vital records indexes (online) of birth records, adoption records, marriage records and death records. Each state is different. Some state records are available before others, why? Because the states formed at different times. In the beginning, there were only thirteen and now there are fifty! That statement may seem trite, but it is easy to forget why you cannot find records of the state you need to search—until you are reminded it was not yet born the year you are searching.

For instance, Oklahoma birth and death records are on file with the State Department of Health—but not before 1900, because Oklahoma did not become a state until 1907. Note: Different states have different rules. Oklahoma will only release birth certificates to the **person** or the **parent** of the person named, and—if you qualify—they are about $15 each. Death records are available from October 1908 at the same cost. Some birth and death records prior to 1908 may be found at the Oklahoma Historical Society. Marriage and divorce records are on file with the clerk of the court in the county where the event occurred. Records are stored differently in each state and prices are subject to change.

More Places to Look

Also, there are many sources of records to help you with your search. Some you may find at home, like in your family Bible. Other items you may locate with relatives you interview. These may include birth certificates, baptismal records, baby books, wedding books, old letters, autograph albums, tombstones, cemetery records, old insurance papers and Social Security cards, newspaper clippings, obituaries, deeds, abstract of titles, wills, tax records, diaries, journals, scrapbooks, military records, letters, pictures, receipts, passports, and school records.

Once you have gone as far as you can go on your own, there are many written records which report an event at, or close to, the time it happened.

Where to Find Other Records

Once you have exhausted the source materials you find at home, you are ready for the next step. Vital records, usually kept by a civil authority, can give you a more complete picture of your ancestor, help you distinguish between two people with the same name, and direct you to a new generation.

In general, these vital records—birth, death, marriage and divorce—were required to be kept in the United States after 1900. These primary source records mark the milestones of our lives and are the foundation of family history research.

Birth certificates with the parent's full names, the name of the baby, the date of the birth and the county where the birth took place are probably in county or state health departments. However, at this time in Oklahoma only the person themselves can get a copy of the birth certificate—and in rare cases when you verify you already know every bit of information on the certificate, then they may provide you a copy.

Marriage records, usually found in county courthouses in the area where your ancestor married, could show the names and birthplaces of each partner's parents. If **divorced**, those records would list the names of the couple's minor children.

Death certificates usually reveal the burial place and give the name and relationship of the person who reported the death.

A date of death and some other information can be found on the Social Security Death Index (SSDI), which is free and online.

https://search.ancestry.com/search/db.aspx?dbid=3693

The Social Security Administration Death Master File contains information on millions of deceased individuals with United States Social Security numbers whose deaths were reported to the Social Security Administration. Birth years for the individuals range from 1875 to last year. Information in these records includes name, birth date, death date, and last known residence. Before the 20th century it is more difficult to locate the records, except in New England or some of the Eastern states. Go ahead and try, you never know what you might receive. Some county courthouses have a death register, but this custom differs even within the same state. Wills or probate records will often give you a date of death or at least a year. Sometimes a statement about the date of death will be found in land or tax records.

Birth Certificate from 1779

TRUE STORY: I wrote to the town clerk of Tunbridge, Orange County, Vermont, and they sent me a birth certificate for my third great-grandmother, Triphena Stedman, who was born there in 1779. Her father, Alexander Stedman, my fourth great-grandfather, was the town clerk and he signed the certificate. What a treasure! You can contact officials by query letter, but they are busy people. You may need to go search in person and you will learn a lot more that way, too. Family history searches are a great excuse to travel.

Want to Buy Your Family's Coat of Arms?

Be leery of anyone wanting to sell you a family coat of arms. The rules for determining who is eligible to display a family crest are very similar to the rules for becoming King or Queen of England. However, even the proper heir cannot display the coat of arms until that person is confirmed by the heraldic authority.

Coats of arms came into general use by feudal lords and knights in battle in the 12th century. By the 13th century, arms had spread beyond their initial battlefield use to become a flag or emblem for families in the higher social classes of Europe, inherited from one generation to the next. Exactly who had a right to use arms, by law or social convention, varied to some degree between countries.

Some nations still maintain the same heraldic authorities which have traditionally granted and regulated arms for centuries and continue to do so in the present day.

There are hundreds of companies who want to sell you your family coat of arms on a tee-shirt, mug, or a "handsomely engraved" plaque. The crests look nice and make great conversation starters, but most likely have nothing to do with your family.

Figure 32: Royal Coat of Arms of the United Kingdom of Great Britain and Northern Ireland.

Buyer Beware!

Coats of arms were usually granted to individuals, not families or surnames, and should be used only by the male line descendants of the person to whom the coat of arms was originally granted. After that one person is deceased, his eldest heir may apply for the same coat of arms. Again, when that person dies, his eldest heir may apply.

When knights were encased in armor, the practice of painting an insignia of honor on their shield became an easy method of distinguishing them. Originally these were granted only to individuals but were afterward made hereditary in England by King Richard I, during his crusade to the Holy Land.

Exactly who had a right to use arms, by law or social convention, varied to some degree between countries. In the German-speaking regions both the aristocracy and burghers (non-noble free citizens) used arms, while in most of the rest of Europe they were limited to the aristocracy. The use of arms spread to the clergy, to towns as civic identifiers, and to royally chartered organizations such as universities and trading companies.

One company prefaces the sale items of one reputable seller of the crests with these three statements:

1) "The specific individual to whom the original coat of arms was granted normally is generally unknown to us, as this is rarely on record in our source books.

2) "Coats of arms are sometimes inaccurately called family crests. We sometimes use these terms interchangeably to better serve our customers."

3) "Our surname history complements a genealogical search–we do not provide a genealogy of a specific family."

In Summary

- ✓ Record enough information about each source so someone else can retrieve the information—also, so you could easily verify your own info.
- ✓ Primary sources are records created at or near the time of an event.
- ✓ Secondary sources are records created a significant amount of time after an event occurred, or by a person who was not present at the event.
- ✓ Vital records record life's "vital" events.
- ✓ Coats of arms were granted to individuals, not families or surnames.

Figure 33: Design your own!
Coats of arms (real ones) are granted to individuals, not families or surnames, and may rightfully be used only by the male line descendants of the person to whom the coat of arms was originally granted.

CHAPTER EIGHT

Getting Organized

Get a handle on the papers.

Successful genealogy research depends upon being able to find needed information again and again. To do so you need a simple system for organizing paper copies of family group records, pedigree charts, documents, notes and research material.

Get a handle on those mounds of papers, books, and scraps. Keep them organized with color-coded files, folders, binders and your computer.

What to Do with All Those Papers?

I started with one three-ring binder and one cardboard filing box with plain manila file folders and hanging files. That soon expanded to two binders, one for maternal ancestors and one for paternal ancestors. A few short years later I added two more, one for each of the four grandparents. Now I have some forty or more three-ring binders and several four-drawer filing cabinets in the garage.

As you collect more and more data, you will benefit from one of the many computer genealogy programs available, such as Legacy, Roots Magic, or one of the many others available for computers. Some are even free. Reunion by

Leisterpro is rated highest for the Macintosh Computer, but there are many more.

As stacks of papers grow, you will need a filing cabinet and file folders to keep separated all those paper copies of the individuals and generations. I encourage you to buy a scanner and go paperless before you kill too many trees. Confession time: I try to go paperless but don't really trust digital files alone. If it is important info, I put it in writing. (note: it is all important.

You probably work mostly with digital files and also scan many records along the way, but some original paper documents you'll want to keep "as is." You can organize such information in many ways, but before you decide what method suits you best, sort through what you have, and type up a list of the items on your computer. Being able to view the documents in front of you in list form will make it easier to devise appropriate categories, such as family groups, vital records, letters, journals, maps, and censuses. The list will help you decide what you need to keep or can discard. Save that electronic list and make a habit of adding to it on an ongoing basis.

Figure 34: Binders for your Family Group Sheets (FGS).

Include appropriate documentation information with that data for easy access. Documents that you want to keep, but don't wish to three-hole punch, can be added in clear plastic sleeves. Buy archival material for storing that will not harm your old documents. You can buy acid-free products at most office supply stores or hobby type stores. Backup materials go in the four-drawer filing cabinets with one drawer for each grandparent line.

You can start with one binder to hold the family history sheets and research materials for your four grandparents. Soon enough you will need to divide your maternal ancestors and paternal ancestors. Later you will need a binder for each of your four grandparents, then your great-grandparents need their own space, and so on. When the surname changes you will need to start a new notebook.

Organizing the Clutter

Ask a group of genealogists how they organize their files and you're likely to get a different answer from each one.

Most folks input the paper data into their computer. Even after you do this, you still need to coordinate the original hard copy documentation you've collected. If you don't have an empty filing cabinet, you don't have to go out and buy one. A cardboard box will work just fine. You can buy document storage boxes, sometimes called bankers boxes, at your local office supply store. You also need hanging files, which fit the boxes perfectly and the hangers slide on the box sides. You definitely need file folders. If you've scrounged some old folders from an office, then you need new file folder labels also. A marking pen will do fine for marking the tabs. If you ever want to use the folder for something other than what you have marked on the tab, just use a file folder label to cover up the old name.

Here are the essentials you need to organize all those papers: box or file drawer, file folders, hanging files to hold the file folders, a marking pen, sticky labels, and perseverance to see the job through. The perseverance is the most important item.

Take a moment each time a new record comes in to file it properly. If you don't take that minute to file the record immediately, you will spend an hour looking for it later.

A Better Way; Color Coding by Family Line

If you have the money to purchase new office supplies, get colored file folders for the lineages of each of your four grandparents. All folders created for the ancestors of one grandparent will be the same color and will be easier to find in the file cabinet.

Colored, letter-size file folders in blue, green, red, and yellow. These are only a little more expensive than the standard manila folders. Put your colored file folders into **Standard green hanging files** with reinforced tops to last through heavy use. Even better, invest in matching color-coded hanging folders.

- **Pens** with an ultra-fine point and black acid-free ink.
- **Highlighters** in light blue, light green, yellow, and pink. Colored pencils also work.
- **Labels for file folders with** blue, green, red and yellow strips along the top and permanent adhesive on the back.
- **Hang the files** in alphabetical order in your file box or cabinet drawer by color, placing the blues alphabetically in one group, greens in another group, etc.
- When your box or file drawer gets full, start another box, keeping the same colors together.
- Binders; Start with one binder for your completed Family Group Sheets (FGS) and research materials and add binders as you fill them up.

Keep piling the family mound into a tree. If you have accumulated a lot of notes and photocopies, you may need to further subdivide the filing, keeping in mind your purpose of making it easier for you to find what you are looking for.

By Surname - All papers for an individual surname are filed together choosing one color for each grandparent line.

By Location - Papers are further broken down by country, state, county, or town to reflect your ancestor's migration.

In Summary:

- ✓ You want to organize your genealogy research material so that you have these benefits:
- ✓ Quick access to genealogical documents, notes, and research you have already gathered.
- ✓ A place to put new documents and notes so you can easily find them again.
- ✓ A filing method to match your computer genealogy program files.

CHAPTER NINE

Posting Queries

Looking for someone.

Once you complete these preliminaries and run out of relatives to interview, move on to established records to verify and expand on what you have.

For instance, you can contact the postmaster of the town where relatives once lived to see if anyone by the same surname is still around.

Find a complete stranger!

TRUE STORY: When my Dad died, we thought he was the last of his family. Then we remembered at one time Dad had mentioned some cousins coming from a little town named Beardsley in Minnesota. They were somehow related to Alpha, the grandfather who had died before I was born. Dad thought they were connected with the family of Joseph Branch, a great uncle.

I addressed an envelope:

c/o Postmaster, Beardsley, MN 56211

I enclosed a Family History Sheet and scribbled a note on the envelope that said: "Please hand this letter to any member or relative of the Joseph Branch family who may still live in the area."

I did not yet know that Joseph Branch had been dead more than fifty years, or I might not have sent the letter.

Within a month I received a note from the postmaster saying no person by the name of Branch still lived there; however, he did happen to know a person related to the Joseph Branch family.

I wrote again, asking the postmaster to please hand that relative the letter. We waited patiently for an answer. One month went by, two months. The heat of summer turned to cool evenings of autumn, snow fell, and then spring arrived.

One day there was an unexpected knock on the door.

It was the "relative of Joseph Branch." He turned out to be Joseph Branch's great grandson—our third cousin.

That family in Minnesota was uneasy about writing to a stranger so they came to Oklahoma to check us out and meet in person. They brought with them a photo album with pictures from the previous century, letters written by my ancestors, and family stories I had never heard before. That was the beginning of a long friendship for our two families, with visits at least once a year.

Our newly discovered cousins brought photos of great-great grandparents, great uncles and aunts, family letters and an

Figure 35: A family album from Minnesota with photos.

autograph album signed by my great-grandmother, that we never would have seen if the postmaster had not passed on my letter of inquiry. The cousins took the photo album and letters back home with them and all the historic items have since been lost or destroyed. We do still have the copies I made long ago.

Tips on Posting a Query

Sometimes you can find distant relatives who may also be researching your family line by posting queries in genealogical publications in the area where your ancestor lived. Go online to www.cyndislist.com where you will find mailing lists targeted to every imaginable location and special interest all over the world.

Focus on posting a separate query for each individual surname or family. Every state and most counties have a genealogical publication and almost all include a section for posting queries. You don't have to join the society to use their contact format although there are benefits to be received from that. Send a query with who, where, when, and what you are seeking about your ancestors. If there is a charge for publication, they will let you know.

Make sure your first line clearly reflects the information you are seeking. Just "need help" won't get as many good results as a subject heading containing a surname, approximate date, and location. Letting people know where you have already checked for information will help to reduce unnecessary suggestions.

Mailing Lists Online

Mailing lists are interactive email forums free for you to subscribe to and participate in. Rootsweb.com hosts thousands of mailing lists with tens of thousands of subscribers. Click on the surname, country, state, or county you are interested in, and browse that mailing list as long as you wish.

If you decide to join so you will be notified of all the queries and answers posted there, be sure to keep a copy of the welcome message that you receive. This message will contain details about the mailing list, the administrator or person who runs the list, with instructions you will need if you want to unsubscribe.

Composing a Query Letter

Letters or emails are preferable to phone calls for querying. This allows the person time to consider the information you need and does not intrude on their activities. A typed letter is easier to read. Don't forget to check your spelling, grammar and punctuation so you will make a good impression. Keep it simple.

Whether writing to a repository or a long-lost cousin, a concise letter will bring better results, briefly explaining your interest as a family member. Keep it short, one page if possible, and make only one request per letter. Be sure the envelope is addressed to the right person and place. Make it as easy as possible for them to help you. Enclose a self-addressed stamped envelope for their reply. This envelope is known in the business as a SASE. Be sure you have the right amount of postage on both envelopes, and a check or money order to cover any anticipated cost.

Enclose family group sheets to help them determine what you need. Add an "enclosure" list after your signature for both you and the recipient. Include your complete address and contact info. Be patient. They may carry the letter for a long time before deciding to answer.

Sending an Email Query

Be tactful and considerate. Explain why you want the information. Make your questions easy to answer. Don't give long-winded tales of your family's exploits, just ask for what you need as specifically as possible.

Focus your query on one name and shoot for the target, rather than listing anything and everything at once. Giving too much unrelated information might scare them off.

Stay away from using abbreviations and acronyms. Others may not be familiar with those abbreviations and may hesitate to reply even though they may actually have information to share.

Typing in all capital letters is usually considered shouting, except on the surname of the person you are asking about which should be capitalized; e.g., COZINE instead of Cozine.

Offer to share your information, citing your sources. Keep a log of letters and emails sent and responses received. Read through your query at least once before sending it. Did you include all pertinent information? Does it make sense? Is it easy to read?

Be sure to thank anyone who responds, whether the information is helpful or not. If someone does a lookup for you, it would be gracious of you to offer to return the favor. If they don't need a lookup done in your county, you might do something nice in their honor, such as a cemetery or newspaper lookup.

Provide full information on how to contact you. Include your name, complete email address, postal service address, and phone. Surprisingly, not everyone uses email. If your query is printed and given to someone who is not computer literate, or if your email address changes as they sometimes do, the researcher will not be able to get in contact with you.

Few family historians are as persistent as the one mentioned in the **true story** that follows. If you are hesitant to use your street address, rent a postal box.

Be patient, keep calm and carry on

TRUE STORY: Just recently I received an answer from a query posted EIGHT years before. My email address had changed over the years, but this determined genealogist was able to track me down.

Here is what he wrote:

"I hope you don't mind that I tracked you down. I suspected your eight-year-old AOL email address, Buffalo234@aol.com, which you were using back then, might no longer be valid and sure enough that email bounced. I googled "Buffalo234" and finally found your twitter page, which led me to your web site and the "contact me" option. Thank goodness!"

Examples of a query to post

The best headings have a name and date of birth, marriage or death. The name of a spouse in the query helps identify the specific ancestor you are looking for. If you don't know the spouse's name, you may be able to list the parent or a child.

SMITH family of New Jersey, PA and Ohio

Stephen SMITH, born in Sussex County, New Jersey, May 6, 1771, died in Meigs Co, OH, 24 March 1841. His wife, Mary (maiden name unknown), born in Sussex Co, NJ, 18 June 1773, died in Meigs county, OH, 23 August 1858. Stephen & Mary's first nine children also born Sussex Co, NJ. Stephen SMITH and family moved to Uniontown, Fayette Co, PA in 1809 and to Meigs County, OH in 1823. Early obituaries claim Stephen SMITH's father died while serving under George Washington, and that Mary SMITH's father furnished horses for the Colonial army. However, since we cannot locate a first name for Stephen's father and cannot identify Mary's surname, no one can join DAR on this line. Their children's names are: Sarah "Sally" (1789-1828), Adonijah (1796-1881), William (1798-1880), Furman (1799-1815), Josiah L. (1800-1891), John Axford (1802-1866), Elizabeth (1806-1893), Mary S. (1808-ca1900), James Adams (1810-1896), Stephen (1812-1815), Isaac W. (1813-1897), Joseph Vandrite (1816-1894), Robert (1817-1822). Would like to learn name of Stephen Smith's

father, and Mary's maiden name and parents. Contact me at:
carolynleonard@me.com or by U.S. mail.

Note: The more common a name your individual has, such as SMITH, the more identifying facts you need to include.
Here is an example of a concise query:

Searching for information on Thomas H. B. COZINE, born 1845 Mercer Co, KY, died after 1885 in Missouri. Contact me at carolynleonard@me.com or by mail.

In Summary

Genealogy queries are an effective way to find others who are researching the same family names you are, and to help you share information with them. A query is basically an advertisement for contact with anyone searching for the same or related ancestors. Queries may be submitted to genealogy magazines, newspapers, or web sites.

Be sure to include these five items in your query.

- Surname you are searching, in all caps.
- Additional surname of spouse, if known.
- Dates of birth, death, marriage, etc, if known.
- Locality of person you are searching.
- Contact info for yourself.

And remember these rules for queries:

✓ ABC - Always Be Courteous.
✓ Follow basic correspondence rules.
✓ Print a copy for your files.

- ✓ Keep a log of queries sent, with date.
- ✓ Always include a name, a locality, and a time period.
- ✓ State exactly what information you need.
- ✓ Limit each query to one family name.
- ✓ No abbreviations, or very few.
- ✓ Type or print. Have someone proofread, if possible.
- ✓ Include your contact info.
- ✓ Be patient. It might be years before you get a hit.

CHAPTER TEN

Spelling Doesn't Count

What's in a Name?

A family name, or surname, is the legal tag by which we are all identified now. This is a legal requirement almost everywhere in the world, but it was not always so. In the 1600s when my Low Dutch ancestors first came from the Netherlands to the new country, some had only one name. Later when the English took charge and New Amsterdam became New York, the Dutch were required to choose a family name.

Most surnames evolved from one of four general sources: a man's occupation, location, father's name, or a physical characteristic. John may be a baker and in his village he would be known as John de (the) baker. This name would eventually become John Baker. The often-found surname prefix "Van" is Dutch for "from." Abram born in Wyck, became Abram Van Wyck.

Patronymics

Patronymics is a naming system where all the children receive an individual first name and then take the first name of their father as a sort-of-surname, so the family name changed with each generation. The child took the father's given name with son, sen, or an s added as a middle name; i.e. Peter Jacobson/Jacobsen/Jacobs.

A type of patronymics existed even in Bible times, Simon bar Jonah meant Simon, son of Jonah. The term "van" would be followed by his nativity, as in Jesus of Nazareth. My ancestor Cosyn Gerritsen Van Putten was Cosyn, son of Gerrit, from Putten in Gelderland, a province in the Netherlands. Putten still exists as an old village which was along the coast of the Zuiderzee. Eventually his sons took the surname of Cosyn—with various spellings of course.

In the case of Jan (John) Cornelsen, father of a husky family of four sons, Jan's sons Pieter, Hans, Hendrick, and Garret would all have the second name of Jansen. There was no continuity of family surnames. For instance, when the son Peter became a father his children would have the second name of Petersen, while the children of his brother Hans would have a family name of Hansen, and Garret's boys would be Garretsons. The name Jansen would disappear from this family in the second generation.

In Western Europe patronyms were common for a time and later became confined to Scandinavian countries. Once established, family names remain an essential part of everyone's personal history. The story of their evolution is important to family history and fascinating in its own right. Formed from first names, place names, nicknames, and occupations, surnames allow us to trace the movements of our ancestors from the Middle Ages to the present day.

Surnames were introduced into England by the Norman barons. Only a few of these barons possessed hereditary surnames in Normandy before the Conquest in 1066, and in most cases such names went back no more than a generation or two. (See *Family Names and Family History* by David Key, published by Continuum International Publishing Group.)

TRUE STORY: The fighters invading England's coast with William the Conqueror came from many lands. Ralph de Braunche (Ralph of Braunche) is identified with the community of St. Denis de Braunche in Pays de Caux, Normandy, on the north side of the Seine not too far from Le Havre. The book, Battle Abbey Roll, documents a list of

William the Conqueror's companions and remains preserved at Battle Abbey, in England.

Because of his support of William the Conqueror, Ralph de Braunche was granted land at Gresham in United Kingdom (UK). He was knighted and entitled to the prefix "Sir" before his name. Although each generation of this progression is not completely proven, it is believed that privilege passed to his son Richard de Braunche born around 1140 at Gresham, to Richard's son William de Braunche, born about 1170, and the privilege passed on to William's son, Sir Peter de Braunche, born about 1200 in Gresham UK.

At that point, the family name issue becomes even more interesting. Sir Peter de Braunche had two sons, Nicholas and Roger.

Nicholas and his descendants carried the name of Braunche, and Roger chose the name de Gresham, for the village where he lived and where his son, also named Roger de Gresham, lived in 1313. (The Norman People and their existing descendants in the British Dominions and the USA, published in 1874 and available online.) So far, we have no indisputable proof.

So much for the English.

A Rose by Any Name Smells Just as Sweet

Be prepared for names to change and evolve into something entirely different. Don't get hung up on spelling.

Dutch names seem especially unpredictable. For instance, the name Vanarsdale must have at least a dozen different known variables. Examples: VanArsdale, Van Arsdalen, Vanosdel, Vanorden, Van Ordon, Vanorsdale, Vann Ausdell, VanArsdall, VanArder, Vanarsdall, Van Norsdell, Van Norsdall, Van Aersdaelen, Van Nosdall, Fenosdal, Fenorsdall, Fanosdol, Van Ausdall, Vananglin, Van Ansdale, Van Orsdel. Recently I received a query from JoAnn "VanAertsdalen," thereby providing even one more spelling option.

Name spellings weren't standardized several generations ago, and many people spelled their own name in a variety of ways. In addition, many people couldn't write, and those who wrote for them when the need arose sometimes had minimal spelling skills. They just spelled phonetically, writing down what they heard.

As you start searching old legal documents and censuses, it is important to be prepared for those differences.

Using Soundex And Miracode Indexes

If you are using Ancestry.com to check the census and have no luck, you may want to click on the option to use Soundex.

When reading microfilm or searching the printed indexes manually, you can use a system based on the way a surname sounds rather than how it might be spelled by the census taker.

To use the Soundex to locate information about a person, you must know his or her full name and the state or territory in which he or she lived at the time of the census. It is also helpful to know the full name of the head of the household in which the person lived, because census takers recorded information under that name.

Surnames that sound the same but are spelled differently, like Smith and Smyth or Neigh and Nay or some other similar sounding names, have the same code and are filed together. This facilitates finding a surname even though it may have been recorded under various spellings. The Soundex coding system was developed in four of the U.S. Census indexes: 1880, 1900, 1910, and 1920.

The codes consist of the first letter of the surname followed by a three-digit code. In the Soundex system, Johnson, Janzen, Johanson, and Jansen are coded as the same name—they're all J525. In somewhat the same manner, surname spellings have evolved.

While it's no longer necessary to code each surname by hand, knowing how surnames are coded helps you understand the system. Soundex aids genealogists by identifying spelling variations for a given surname.

You can use a Soundex converter free at the website for Rootsweb.com on the Internet. Web addresses change, although you can always find it with a search in your browser.

Know About Transcribing Mistakes

When checking the census, even on Ancestry or Heritage Quest, try every possible combination of letters before giving up. The transcribers may have confused an L for an S or some other letter. The handwriting of some census takers was atrocious!

TRUE STORY: Researchers had been unable to locate either Solomon Large or his father Thomas Large in an early census. After diligent work the missing persons were found. Solomon had been incorrectly listed as Slamon Lag, and the Thomas Large entry was found indexed under "S—" transcribed wrongly as Sarge.

In Summary

- ✓ Most surnames evolved from one of four general sources: a man's occupation, location, father's name or physical characteristic.

- ✓ Don't get hung up on how a name is spelled when determining family relationships.

- ✓ Be aware of possible spelling errors when researching census or other records that may have been transcribed incorrectly.

CHAPTER ELEVEN

Tiptoe through the Tombstones

The cemetery search technique.

Search for your ancestors in cemetery and obituary listings, going in person to the burial ground if possible. You should always notice the names on nearby graves, as they are probably relatives also.

At any local library, and online as well, you can usually find cemetery indexes with a listing of the burials recorded. Why would you need to visit the cemetery if you already have a death date? Because you may learn many other things while you are there. Usually whole families are buried close together. Many communities still decorate family graves late in the month of May. Once known as Decoration Day on May 30, Memorial Day is now an official holiday on the last Monday of May, although mostly focused on military veterans. If you go then, you may meet new relatives visiting your family graves.

You probably never noticed the variety of cemeteries before. Watch for small family graveyards, large burial grounds in cities, abandoned rural graveyards, religious affiliation burial grounds, churchyards, and even older churches where people were buried inside or under the floor. Often people were buried on or near land they once owned.

Study the stones

Once you find your ancestor's grave, a close study of the stone may give you more clues to follow, such as a Masonic symbol or veteran's organization emblem.

Thousands of different religious and secular symbols are found on tombstones, indicating attitudes towards death and the hereafter, membership in a fraternal or social organization, or an individual's trade, occupation or even ethnic identity.

Learning about the symbolism and variety of tombstone art can become a hobby of its own. Many of the elaborate markers erected in the nineteenth century were styled after ancient Greek or Roman memorials. While many of these symbols may appear to have a hidden meaning, we cannot always know for sure what our ancestors were trying to say. They may have included a particular icon only because they thought it was attractive.

TRUE STORY: There are six identical gravestones in our family plot for my grandparents and their three adult sons. Each stone has a stalk of wheat and the inscription *"A haven of rest is my Lord."* I read that wheat, as a symbol, on a tombstone meant "ripe for harvest". I asked my dad about the meaning. He said his mother chose the first stone and symbols to mark the grave of her husband, his dad. She chose that symbol for two reasons. Her man was a farmer and secondly, because she liked the way it looked. The other five family members simply followed her lead.

Always Ask Permission

Always ask permission to go on private property if you are searching in abandoned cemeteries. Different states have different rules about access and upkeep. An older person or historian in a nearby community may have information about your relative who was interred in an abandoned cemetery.

If the burial ground is still maintained, go to the nearest town hall to learn the name of the sexton or the person responsible for upkeep. That person probably has lived in the community a long time and may be able to give you information.

In a small cemetery the caretaker may do everything from digging the graves to keeping the records and cutting the grass. The sexton records may include information such as when the lots were purchased, who paid for it, and how many are buried there. At one large cemetery I visited, the sexton keeps an office on the grounds. At another rural burial ground, the sexton stores his card files at his home. At another there were no card files at all. The caretaker's only designated responsibility was to mow the grass, but he actually still knew all the families of the people buried there.

TRUE STORY: My great uncle Levi Branch was lost. He died in 1913 and was not buried with his parents, nor was his grave found with his five children who died as infants in Wayne County, Illinois. His widow's grave was known to be in Kansas and Levi was not there, either. I finally found his death certificate in the courthouse at Centralia in Marion County, Illinois. The death certificate said Levi died of bronchial tuberculosis and was buried in City Cemetery. (Reference Book 14 page 126.)

That would be great information, except there is no burial ground in Centralia named "city cemetery," and there never has been, so far as anyone there could remember.

With the help of the Elmwood Cemetery Sexton in Centralia, Illinois, almost a century after his death, in a cemetery covering more than sixty acres of burials, we found him. Hallelujah!

After many phone calls to different places, the town clerk said Elmwood had always been the city's cemetery. The records, the clerk said, burned in 1925 and she had no records of it being called by any name other than Elmwood but that must be the right one. She gave me the name of the sexton, but he was off duty that day. We drove to the address for Elmwood. We gave up the search after a few hours.

Disappointed, we left Illinois and returned home. Later, I called the caretaker on the phone.

He searched his files and found an old card showing Levi Branch bought a cemetery lot in 1904 for his adult daughter, Ida Elizabeth Branch, and he also purchased six other lots. The caretaker did not know if there were any tombstones on those lots, but he promised if we came back, he would have a map to help us find it.

We drove back to Illinois, and the caretaker kept his promise. We found the correct block in the cemetery. There was a tombstone for Levi and his wife with a separate one for their daughter.

Levi's Civil War military marker was also there, although almost buried under the years of soil.

Uncle Levi was no longer lost.

Figure 36: Finding Uncle Levi.

Funeral Home Records

Learn the names and addresses of local morticians. Funeral-home records often have information not available elsewhere, such as where and by whom the lot was purchased. In the records of the mortician's office, you should find the name and address of who paid the bill. For those funeral homes no longer in business, check the local historical society or contact other funeral homes in the area. Perhaps they received the archived records. Sadly, these important historic records were often destroyed instead of being saved.

Follow the Money to Find Your Ancestor

Why do you follow the money? Learning who paid for the last expenses of your ancestor can lead you to a treasure trove of family history.

Cemetery plot deeds are recorded and may give you the married name of a daughter who purchased the lot for great-grandpa. The deed may name the funeral home in charge of burial, and you might even discover an obituary in the file.

How Do You Find Those Old Burial Grounds?

The body was usually buried in the family cemetery, if there was one, or out behind the barn or up on the hill. Comforting words were spoken, and life went on until the next person died. Death, if not a welcome visitor, was a familiar one.

The American Way of Death

For centuries in America, we tended to our dead. People died at home. Relatives lovingly washed and dressed the body, laid it out in the parlor and stayed close by. They sat up with the body all night until the family could gather to bury the body, which usually took place the next day.

The American way of death changed during the Civil War, when others were paid to undertake the job of transporting the bodies of soldiers killed far from home; this is when formaldehyde as an embalming agent was first used. Less than a hundred years ago we began routinely to hand over our dead to strangers called the undertakers.

Soon the elderly infirm as well as most critically ill family members were moved to hospitals to die. Within decades, what had been deemed a family responsibility was turned over to others.

If you ever tried to find a rural cemetery, you will remember hand-drawn maps sketched in pencil on a napkin, U-turns, stops for directions, and sometimes giving up because it had become too dark to take a picture of the stone, by the time you found it.

One little item of technology can cure that problem. A global positioning system (GPS) can get you there in no time if you have the coordinates, no matter how remote the graveyard.

A good place to find cemetery locations for free is on www.cyndislist.com/cemeteries.

Another place is www.findagrave.com. This site currently contains information for more than 280,000 cemeteries in more than 170 different countries, and it is still free, even though now owned by Ancestry.com. Sometimes the person administrating the memorial for your ancestor may have posted an obituary on the site, or other information to help you with your research.

Most of the mailing lists for a particular state and county include cemetery information and sometimes show an online index to the burials.

Many of these give the GPS coordinates, as do more and more county records.

What Next? Invest in a GPS

If you have a GPS, that instrument may be able to lead you right to the spot you are looking for. Developed by the U.S. Department of Defense, GPS is a network of satellites that orbit the earth and constantly measure positions. Once very rare, now most travelers carry a portable GPS in their car or have a built-in model. They are standard equipment in many newer automobiles, and most hunters carry hand-held versions. Boats and airplanes have used GPS devices for years, and prices have dropped enough that most family historians have one for their personal use.

My own handheld GPS system includes a locator on the menu under Points of Interest, where I found a welcome heading, *"cemeteries."*

The U.S. Geological Survey (USGS.com), a science agency under the Department of the Interior, produces several sets of maps and a database often valuable for research in genealogy. The Find a Grave forums are currently posting GPS coordinates for as many cemeteries as possible. Once you have a GPS location for a grave or a cemetery, you can locate it on a map as well as on the earth.

Google Earth (https://www.google.com/earth/) is a great tool to combine with GPS. Find the coordinates of the cemetery, and then go to Google Earth to find the nearest intersections to feed into your GPS.

Another place for cemetery information with a long, long name is the United States Geological Survey, Geographic Names Information (USGS, GNIS). (http://geonames.usgs.gov/). From that site you can click on Google Maps on the right-hand side of the web page to learn street names and the latitude/longitude coordinates for your GPS.

High-Tech Hide and Seek

Purchasing a GPS for yourself may lead you to combine two popular hobbies—genealogy and geocaching. GPS technology is creating high tech games in this century. Geocaching is a high-tech treasure hunting game played throughout the world by adventure seekers equipped with GPS devices. The basic idea is to locate hidden containers, called geocaches, outdoors. Once found, the geocache is opened and noted. The find is shared online. People from all age groups enjoy geocaching.

How do you choose the perfect GPS device for you? Prices might range from under $100 for a basic handheld device to $1,000 or more for a souped-up version connected to your laptop or PDA. The best ones come with some type of mapping software such as the "maps and streets" program.

For our genealogy trips I bought a small handheld GPS we could use on foot, and a larger one for the car. Both units came with a charger that plugs into the cigarette lighter, and they both offer voice guidance. However, it is always best to have someone other than the driver monitoring the unit.

GEOCACHING: We learned about geocaching while on our own treasure hunt for the tiny abandoned cemetery where my great-grandmother Caroline is buried in Missouri.

TRUE STORY: Just off I-44 and old highway 66 in the tiny town of Strafford, a suburb east of Springfield, in a small grove of sassafras and maple trees we finally located a dozen or more Civil War period stones still standing, others askew. The little graveyard is not well maintained but is occasionally mowed. A gravel path winds around patches of poison ivy and brambles. We never learned why Caroline is buried here when all the rest of her family is planted in Illinois or Oklahoma. I never drive past without stopping to leave some flowers, or just pay my respects.

Her tombstone says simply, "Mother, Caroline Branch, wife of Samuel C. Branch" and on the curved top is carved "At Rest."

Caroline's grave is off by itself. The marble stone looks newer than the others in the cemetery, although the headstone has fallen and leans against the base, resulting in an open triangular space under the base.

While straightening the headstone we discovered a sealed quart Mason jar, a geocache, containing several trinkets.

A note inside the jar explained the rules of geocaching: "Once you find a geocache, sign the logbook and return the geocache to its original location. Afterward, share your geocaching stories and photos online. If you take something from the geocache, you should leave something of equal or greater value."

Figure 37: Finding a Geocache.

Back at the motel, we found the geocaching instructions online, and learned the "hint" to finding this particular cache at the stated GPS location was "at rest," matching the carving on the top of Caroline's stone.
(http://www.geocaching.com/)

What to Wear and What to Take

Dress appropriately for a cemetery stroll. Wear long pants, long sleeves, and old shoes to ward off the chiggers, ticks, snakes, poison ivy, and tall grass. Take along a can of bug spray, some flowers to leave on the grave, a brush and soft cloth with a jug of water to clean off the dirt, a camera to record the stone and a reflector to reflect and improve readability of the stone.

Some people use white chalk to bring out the lettering though chalk is frowned on by many genealogy organizations. If you do resort to using chalk, please wash it off before leaving. Never use any chemicals or cleaning products as this could damage the carvings.

Take Several Shots

Take at least two photos of each headstone, one close up so you can read the inscription, and one from a distance that identifies the marker's location in the cemetery. You may also want to take a wide-angle shot of the entire family plot. I usually take several pictures from different angles showing most of the cemetery, to give perspective on where the grave is located. I also shoot a photo of the gates or entry. If there is time and the cemetery is small, I take an individual shot of each stone to be put online to help other researchers.

Best Time to Visit & Take Photos

The best time to take pictures is usually an early spring morning with the sun shining on the stone. However, sometimes the afternoon sun casts a shadow just the right way to make the letters easier to read, so go when you can and take as many photos from as many different angles as possible.

Why Do Tombstones Usually Face East?

Traditionally gravestones face east. This east/west orientation is the most common in all parts of the world. Facing east is symbolic of the morning sunrise and new beginnings. Native Americans always place their tipis in a "sacred circle" with the doorway opening to the east. Asian Feng Shui says it is good if the main front door of your home faces east. The front door is considered to be the "mouth" where vital energy enters and exits your home.

The earliest settlers usually buried the deceased with their feet pointing toward the east and the head of the coffin toward the west, ready to rise up and face the "new day." The Bible describes this event as *"the trumpet shall sound and the dead in Christ shall rise."* The body was usually positioned between the headstone and a small footstone, with the inscriptions facing outward. A footstone would be facing east, with the decorated face of the larger headstone facing west.

For some reason the north side of a burial ground became considered less desirable, and often that is the last section of the burying ground to be used. In some cemeteries the north side was set aside for slaves, servants, suicides, travelers, or the "potter's field" where very poor people were placed.

Early burials were seldom in neat rows like we see now. Families did not buy a cemetery plot. Often an area at the homestead or plantation became a family graveyard, or they might be buried in a nearby churchyard. Plots might be reused years later.

TRUE STORY: Finding one of these early family cemeteries can give you new insight into your family. We stopped at the public library in tiny Fortville, Indiana, to research part of the family we knew little about.

I had read online that in 1812 Robert & Anna Stewart Fausset, sometimes found spelled Faucett or even Foset, came west from Virginia. They moved to Indiana by wagon and established a residence "on Lick Creek where it flows into Fall Creek," near Fortville. We found the "Fausset plantation" and the little Fausset Family Cemetery with the help of old county histories and a friendly small-town librarian. One of the stones was for Anna, wife of Robert Fausset and daughter of Robert Stewart. Anna Stewart Fausset was apparently the first one buried there. She died on 24 September 1840 at the age of fifty-two.

According to the item in the Hamilton County history book, Robert Fausset built a water-powered saw mill, corn mill and kilns on Lick Creek where they made their own brick, and the old millrace was still standing in the 1950s. The first road surveyed along Fall Creek from Indianapolis to Pendleton ran beside the Fausset plantation with the first school built across the road. Methodist Episcopal religious meetings convened early on at the Fausset home.

The graveyard had been in back of the barn, according to the picture in the history book. The barn is no longer there, but the large house just west of the cemetery had been restored. A new sign marks the well-kept fenced plot with thirty-six marked graves and a wide carriage gate. We spent the afternoon cleaning the stones and indexing the cemetery.

How Old Is the Stone?

One way to determine the era in which your ancestor lived and died is to examine material from which the tombstone is made.

- If your ancestor has a stone made of slate or common fieldstone, chances are the stone dates from 1796-1830.
- If the stone is flat-topped hard marble, dates are about 1830-1849.
- If the "mystery" stone is round or pointed soft marble with cursive inscriptions, look for a date of 1845-1868.
- Masonic four-sided stones began to be seen in 1850 and are still in use today.
- Pylons, columns. and all exotic-style monuments are usually dated 1860-1900.
- Zinc monuments date from 1870-1900.
- Granite, now common, came into use after 1900.

Finding a hidden family cemetery

We got directions from the tiny Fortville library: The cemetery is located between Fall Creek and Lick Creek going west on a little winding road (1075S) from State Road 13 about one mile north of Fortville (Hancock Co) through a densely wooded area of hills and dales.

Figure 38: Fausset family burial ground, originally behind the barn, in Indiana.

Genealogists like me and you love cemeteries!

Cemeteries can be critical for finding information related to the births and deaths of our ancestors. The word "graveyard" primarily refers to a burial ground within a churchyard, so this small place is a recognized cemetery.

Often dozens of stones pile up at the base of a tree. It always makes me want to cry.

Saving the Stone Words

If the writing is too faded to read, and it usually is, then you must resort to desperate measures.

Gravestone Rubbing

Rubbing is what you did as a child when you placed a scrap of paper over a coin and brought up the coin's design by covering the paper with lead pencil strokes. Gravestone rubbing is the same process, where you place paper over the stone and rub However, gravestone rubbing is controversial. Experts at the Association for Gravestone Studies insist you can damage a gravestone just by doing a rubbing. That seems hard to believe, but gravestone rubbing is a practice being banned in some states and many cemeteries.

Figure 39: Stacking Stones
These have been carefully placed against a church foundation.

Bringing Out the Etchings

Some people use shaving cream to bring out the inscriptions, sometimes by first wetting the stone with water. Cover a section of the stone with the cream and use a straight edge like Styrofoam or cardboard to remove the excess. Some say there are chemicals in shaving cream that damages the stone—the same shaving cream that men have been applying for eons to the tender skin of their faces.

Dick Eastman of the Eastman Genealogical Newsletter says the story of damage from shaving cream is a hoax. He says, "I have condoned the use of shaving cream ever since I had a long conversation with a person with a doctorate degree in chemistry who was also a genealogist and had researched the issues. I later had that corroborated by another chemist and verified by the person from the tombstone company."

To read Mr. Eastman's comments go to:

(http://blog.eogn.com/eastmans_online_genealogy/2005/05/tombstones_and_/comments/page/2/#comments)—or just do a search on the keywords.

Reflecting the Light

Another suggestion to bring out the inscriptions for photos sends you to your local department store to pick up a full-length door mirror for around ten bucks. Angle the sunlight so the reflected light shines across the surface of the stone. The light must come from a side angle across the face, forming shadows in the grooves of the letters.

Where Have All the Gravestones Gone?

Grieving families sometimes plant a tree to shade a loved one's grave, never considering what may happen when that tree is fully grown.

You may not have the opportunity to photograph the epitaphs in your family cemetery. Those gravestones might be missing due to vandalism or perhaps nature and age have done the damage. Sometimes rural cemeteries have been allowed to grow up in weeds or become part of a pasture with cattle trampling the graves. People have been known to carry off loose tombstones to use in a building foundation or sidewalk.

Figure 40: A tree eating a tombstone in Kentucky.

Money, Marbles, and Chalk

We sometimes use natural white sidewalk chalk, which is related to the same material as marble, slate, granite, and sandstone. Chalk certainly is not as harmful as acid rain or droppings from a bird that has been eating mulberries—and how do you prevent that? In the many years we have been doing this and returning to visit the same stones again, we have not seen them damaged by the chalk. However, we have seen stones completely disappear or be broken lying face down in the dirt, sometimes buried in sod. Often misplaced stones are found leaning against a tree trunk or tossed along the fence. At those times we are thankful to have preserved a grave marker on film.

Sometimes using a spray bottle of water will work to bring out the letters. You may want to try placing a plastic mirror or some aluminum foil at an angle to reflect the sunlight.

No matter what method you use to take the photos, send a copy to your local genealogical society or place the images online yourself. That way the work will not need to be done by others in the future, and the stone words will be "saved" in case something happens to them later.

Figure 41: Before and after cleaning.

Stories the stones can tell

Once you find their resting place, spend a little time with your ancestors. They want to be remembered, and you are their only hope at the moment. The stones often tell of great sorrow such as the same family burying babies year after year.

After using a soft brush to remove dirt from this stone, we applied natural white sidewalk chalk to bring out the lettering for a permanent record, as an example see Figure 92. Many organizations discourage the use of chalk, but we didn't know it at the time.

Five Tiny Stones

Read and record carefully each stone near your ancestor. Later you may learn these are relatives. When you see the markers of several children who died about the same time, suspect an epidemic such as whooping cough or diphtheria. Tetanus, a dreaded infection in earlier days, took its toll. Whole families also died quickly in 1918 from the Spanish flu epidemic. A young mother with an infant buried beside her would indicate childbirth complications.

TRUE STORY: Almost twenty years to the day, I returned to visit my great-grandfather's grave in rural Illinois. Only then did I recognize the five tiny mounds near him that marked the graves of five grandchildren. Only three markers remained on a later trip, the others having disappeared in the intervening years.

From family legend we knew our great uncle and aunt had a daughter who died young and they had raised an orphan nephew. I did not know until I walked this old graveyard path and cleaned the stones that their first five babies died as infants.

Mary Lorena died 1869 age 3 months
Oren Delbert slipped away in 1870 age 2 months
Joseph V. died 1875 age 3 years
Emma Leota in 1876 age 5 months
Anna Louisa passed in 1878 age 14 months.

These five tiny, identical tombstones stand all in a row bearing silent witness to the difficulty of life in the 19th century. Child number six, Ida Elizabeth, named for her grandmother, was luckier than her siblings. She lived to age 24 and is buried in another town where her parents moved to escape their "bad luck." (See Finding Levi, Chapter 14 of this book.)

The sexton's record listed Ida Elizabeth's cause of death as "consumption," so named because it seemed to consume people from within. Symptoms included a bloody cough, fever, pallor, and long relentless wasting. Doctors considered consumption incurable until 1946 with the discovery of the antibiotic streptomycin. Prior to that, the only treatment besides sending the victim to a sanatorium meant collapsing an infected lung to "rest," a technique of little benefit and largely discontinued by the 1950s. The disease consumption is now known as tuberculosis or TB. Although the disease is still around today, it can be treated with a single antibiotic.

Figure 42: Five tiny stones tell a story.

Since these five youngsters died in different years, it does not appear there was an epidemic. We believe all the siblings died of consumption, which was highly infectious. TB/consumption is spread through the air when people who have the disease cough, sneeze, or spit. These little victims and their parents did not know that back in 1875.

In Summary:

- ✓ First, check online for cemetery index and directions.
- ✓ Get permission to go on private property.
- ✓ Different states have different rules about access.
- ✓ Wear protective clothing and bring bugspray.
- ✓ Take pencil, paper, and camera—and a friend to help.
- ✓ Go on Memorial Day when you may find relatives visiting.
- ✓ When looking for additional family burials, carefully inspect and record nearby stones.
- ✓ Take lots of photos.

CHAPTER TWELVE

Gardens of Art

Finding hidden meaning in stone epitaphs

Cemeteries and graveyards are open-air museums and some of the finest works of art can be seen in old cemeteries. I have visited many cemeteries as a family historian and a genealogist. Young people usually associate these places with death. For me, a visit to a cemetery is similar to visiting an art museum. The better ones—clean, trimmed, and well maintained—are places of beauty and everlasting memorials that celebrate the lives of many individuals. Most burial grounds contain very artistic tombstones, testifying to the talent and skill of the people who changed rocks into works of art, and to those who paid for them.

Cemetery iconology offers the researcher a glimpse of what was important to the person whose life is represented in the stone. We all know what the golden arches mean. Icons, or the carvings on gravestones, were used for a purpose, a type of shorthand. Most carvers charged by the word, so icons carved into the stone saved many hours and therefore, much money.

A handshake symbol on a tombstone usually signifies a welcome into the heavenly world. Some of the most common icons feature pointing index fingers, funerary urns, willow trees, hourglasses and stars, all designed to convey some important message about the family or society's understanding of life at the time.

The draped urn was a well-understood symbol of death or mortality, the urn representing the return of the body back to ashes, as in cremation. The urn might be accompanied by a more hopeful "tree of life" motif, signifying that although the individual perished, the remains of the deceased provide the seed for new life.

The weeping willow, a symbol commonly found from 1660 to 1740, demonstrated the grief and sorrow experienced by survivors of the departed. Cemeteries have had a bad rap.

Figure 43: Examples of tree stump tombstones.

Fear of death, superstition, and reluctance to deal with grief causes people to avoid what they consider a place of sadness. Tiptoeing through the tombstones, you may see beautiful seashells and sun images, rosettes, stars, winged heads, and flowers of every description.

We've visited cemeteries with a park area featuring fountains, goldfish ponds, beautiful flower gardens and shrubbery, like we found in the Lexington, Kentucky, historic graveyard which was established in 1848. The designated historical landmark encompasses 170 acres.

Another scenic cemetery, Evergreen Memorial Park in Colorado, serves a diverse function with a cemetery and funeral home as well as a wedding chapel, living museum, and wildlife preserve. In a world of change and turmoil, cemeteries give us a place to pause and reflect. Going there we feel connected not only with our past but also with the pasts of others.

Usually, the most attention-getting markers represent an insurance company called "Woodmen of the World" (WOW) that provided markers early in the twentieth century. In addition to offering life insurance protection to members, early Woodmen certificates provided for a monument benefit. Originally gravestones were furnished to members free of charge. Later the markers were an extra hundred-dollar option.

Woodmen tombstones vary greatly in size and shape. Some resemble a tree stump, others a stack of cut wood, elaborate hand-carved monuments, simple stones and stake-type markers driven into the ground, each with elements symbolic of Woodmen ceremonies or rituals.

A tree stump standing four to five feet high, based on the Woodmen Society logo, is the most common symbol used on their gravestone designs. During the 1920s the society stopped providing stone markers when the cost of materials increased; however, the unique tree trunk design can still be spotted in many cemeteries in the Midwest.

Woodmen markers were originally intended to be a uniform design, but not all stonecutters followed the design provided by the company. This resulted in many variations reflecting members' personal tastes.

Have you ever walked through a cemetery and wondered about the meanings of the designs carved on old tombstones? Once you do, you'll see cemeteries and grave markers in a different light.

Here are a few symbols to watch for.

Anchor: Hope
Arrow: Mortality
Bed or empty chair: The deathbed
Book: Faith everlasting
Broken column: a break in life
Butterfly: The resurrection
Circle: Eternity
Column: Mortality
Cross: Christianity
Cypress tree: Deep mourning
Dove: The soul, peace
Garland: Purity, innocence
Gates: Heavenly entrance
Hands: Farewell
Hand with finger pointing up: Ascension into heaven
Clasping hands: Masculine & feminine, everlasting union
Heart: Love & devotion
Hourglass: The passage of life
Ivy: Friendship
Labyrinth: The passage of life
Lamb: Innocence
Lamp: Sanctity, the eternal flame dispelling darkness
Laurel: Victory or peace
Lily: Chastity, innocence, and purity
Lion: Resurrection
Obelisk: Eternal life
Palm: Triumph of a martyr over death
Passion Flower: Christ's passion, redemption
Pelican: Charity
Phoenix: Resurrection
Pyramid: Eternity

Rocks: Everlasting strength
Rose: Silence
Scythe or Sickle: Time, the Grim Reaper
Shell: Pilgrimage
Ship: Christianity
Skull: Mortality
Snake: Eternity
Sundial: Passage of time
Sword: Justice or fortitude
Torch: Immortality
Tree: Regeneration or knowledge
Urn: Mortality
Wheat: Fruitfulness, harvest time
Willow: Grief
Yew: Deep mourning

Secret Societies

Many symbols of secret societies, clubs and fraternal organizations may in turn lead you to learn more about your ancestor's life:

AL — American Legion
BSA — Boy Scouts of America
BPOE — Benevolent Protective Order of Elks (Lodge)
CFA — Companions of the Forest of America
DOP — Degree of Pocahontas
DR — Daughters of Rebekah (IOOF Auxiliary)
OES — Order of Eastern Star (Masonic Auxiliary)
FB — Fraternal Brotherhood
FOE — Fraternal Order of Eagles (Lodge)
FOE Auxiliary — Spouse of an Eagle
GAR — Grand Army of the Republic (Union Civil War)
IOOF — Independent Order of Odd Fellows (Lodge)
IORM — Improved Order of Red Men
KP — Knights of Pythias
KC or K of C — Knights of Columbus (Catholic)
KOTM — Knights of the Maccabees
LOOM — Loyal Order of Moose (Lodge)

LOTM — Ladies of the Maccabees
MASON — see below
MWA — Modern Woodmen of America
NOW — Neighbors of Woodcraft
PS — Pythian Sisters
RG — Rainbow Girls (Masonic sorority)
SA — Salvation Army
SM — Society of Mary (Catholic)
TR — Theta Rho Girls (IOOF Sorority)
WOTM — Women of the Moose (Lodge Auxiliary)
WOW — Woodmen of the World

Other symbols to watch for:

- The Knights of Pythias features the letters FCB for Friendship, Charity, Benevolence
- The IOOF icon is almost always shown with letters FLT for Friendship, Love, & Truth
- Symbols for the Masonic Lodge are many and varied. Masons /Freemasons /AAONMS, AASR, AF&AM, F&AM, IGGCRSM, K of M, RAM.

Attn: Check the Masonic archives

Several of America's founding fathers were Masons and placed their Rosicrucian and Freemasonry symbol on the US dollar bill. You may find any of these symbols on a gravestone, which signals you to check Masonic archives. The primary symbol of the Masons is the square and compass, often with the letter G in the center. Another symbol of this lodge is the all-seeing eye, as is noted above at the top of the pyramid on each $1 bill.

What's a Maiden's Garland?

I have never seen a Maiden's Garland, apparently used frequently on grave markers in England. The symbol represented a garland of white paper or linen, embellished with streamers and a single white glove, carried at the funerals of unmarried women of blameless reputation. The garlands hung in the church after the funeral and were allowed to decay in place. Pieces would be buried in the graveyard.

Now, here's a murder mystery waiting to be written!
Lester Moore at Boothill Cemetery in Tombstone, Arizona, died in a shoot-out:
>
> *Here lies Lester Moore*
> *Four slugs from a 44.*
> *No Les*
> *No More.*

Angels unaware

Nowadays cherubs are more often associated with Valentine's Day, but many cherubs and baby angels can be found on monuments for children.

Angels gazing skyward, pointing meaningfully to the heavens, clasping wreaths, or even lying across the grave became so popular that vast quantities were shipped from Italy. Angel statues and angel figures are often frequently found as grave markers, but the most unusual angel statue I have ever seen is the legendary weeping angel.

TRUE STORY: The West State Street Cemetery in Athens, Ohio, is home to the *Angel of the Unknown Dead*. The monument, dedicated in 1924, commemorates all unknown soldiers and others unknown buried there. The little fenced cemetery is near Ohio University campus, oldest public university in Ohio, first one in the Northwest Territory and the ninth oldest public university in the entire United States. Organizers founded the university in 1804, and burials in the cemetery probably date from then.

Many ghost stories associated with Athens and the University are centered around the former Athens Lunatic Asylum. Legendary are the horrors, such as lobotomies, that supposedly went on there from 1874 to 1993. As an aside, according to the annual report in 1876, the leading cause of insanity among the male patients was masturbation.

But ... back to the mysterious weeping angel.

Figure 44: Masonic Symbols.

Many who pass by the angel say they've seen her wings flutter. Others claim they saw her shed real tears. She does have a sad appearance with eyes downcast and shoulders slumped. People claim to see strange lights, orbs, and mist while visiting this cemetery at night. They also say she cries real tears after sundown each Sunday. I would not know, because we left before the sun went down.

The Judge of Athens County

My ancestor is buried near the Weeping Angel at the old State Street Cemetery.

TRUE STORY: Alexander Stedman, a native of Vermont who became a judge when he immigrated to the new state of Ohio, had three wives. Not all at once, of course. The west was hard on women – as Alice Marriot's famous book title says, *The West was Hell on Horses, and Women.*

Alexander Stedman's gravestone includes a memorial to his first wife, Sarah (Cushman) Stedman, who died in 1802.

Judge Stedman's second wife, the widow Comfort (Hatch) Crippen, lived only a year or two after her marriage to Judge Stedman. She is believed buried in a rural cemetery, the old James Crippen graveyard at Guysville in Athens Co. where many of the early pioneers are buried.

In 1806 at the age of 58, the Judge married third, the young, never-married Sarah "Sally" Jones. He died eight years later. The now-broken marker for Sally, who died in 1818, recorded the remark: "*Last* wife of Alexander Stedman."

The funeral for Sally must have been fun. In the estate papers at the University library we found her last expenses included: 1 gal. French brandy & 2 b. (two barrels?) of whiskey, half pound loaf sugar and cinnamon, pint of French brandy, two jars French brandy, and a fourth pound of tea.

The inventory and sale of Sally (Jones) Stedman, deceased, did not mention any brandy or whiskey, so it must have been consumed by grieving friends at the wake.

Field Stones and Unmarked Graves

At almost every burial ground you will find many unmarked graves, and some that *appear* unmarked. Look closely; many of those burial places may actually be marked with a flat or upright fieldstone. In other cases, no commercial marker was ever placed, although the family knew and honored the grave of their loved one so long as they lived.

During hard economic times the general population simply could not afford to invest in dying while living was such a trial. With a life expectancy of forty years and general illiteracy, there was little point in erecting expensive markers with epitaphs only a few could read.

Those blank fieldstones may memorialize more than a dead body. A barely visible fieldstone marks the grave of the first murder victim in a rural corner.

Only a rough white fieldstone, now almost covered by Buffalo grass sod, marks the grave of the first murder victim in the newly created Oklahoma Territory in 1906. No name or dates are carved there, but the story has been handed down and the victim is not forgotten more than a century later.

To show you the value of court records and archived newspapers, I used them to solve this hundred-year-old cold case murder.

In many cases cemeteries have been vandalized, or simply allowed to grow up in a tangle of weeds and brush. We know of a cemetery in Kentucky where the farmer not only allowed the cattle to pasture through the tombstones, knocking them over and breaking them, and he also tied a tombstone to the back of his tractor and used it to level his ground.

A fieldstone marks the grave of a murder victim

TRUE STORY: Forty-three marked graves fill tiny Goldenrod cemetery east of Buffalo, Oklahoma. Only a small white stone from a nearby field, now barely visible, marks an important burial. Hearing about a murder mystery connected to that stone, I used genealogy research skills to uncover the facts.

Under that fieldstone lies Edward "Scotty" Smith, victim of the first murder in Harper County. Tracing details of the crime reveals a story exciting as any novel. Lead characters include two beautiful young women, two wild bronc bachelors, a suspect who is a third cousin to the famous lawyer Temple Houston and descendent of Texas hero Sam Houston, possible bribery of a judge, and an interesting post-trial decision by the arresting officer and the accused murderess.

According to early court records Edward T. "Scotty" Smith was killed on December 2, 1906. The case is filed in book number one, case number 774, of Woodward County, Oklahoma Territory. The case was first heard on the 29th of February 1908.

The court records are skimpy, and the case jumped back and forth between Woodward and Buffalo. Determining the court of jurisdiction seemed problematic.

The crime occurred in Woodward County, Oklahoma Territory, which soon became Harper County, Oklahoma Territory, and at statehood in November 1907, the Constitutional Convention declared that area to be Harper County in the state of Oklahoma.

The scene of the crime lay in that portion of Woodward County carved off to become Harper County, so the case moved to the county seat of Harper County for trial as the first homicide there. Later the case moved back to Woodward County for a coroner's Jury, then an indictment was filed and set for trial in district court, Woodward.

The first document "Information for Murder" filed in Harper County on February 1, 1908, listed four defendants in the murder of Edward T. Smith on December 2, 1906: Sam Houston, Vesther Ferneau (a woman), Harrison White, and Mary Smith (the victim's widow).

The murder indictment alleged the defendants hit Smith over the head with a club, tied a lariat rope around his neck with the other end secured to the saddle horn on a horse, and dragged the unconscious victim behind the horse a half mile resulting in the man's death. The indictment claimed Smith's wife, assisted by her unnamed "boyfriend" and another couple, conspired to do away with Smith.

Reportedly, Smith and his wife had an argument about going to church. He told her if she went, not to bother coming back. Defiant Mary went anyway. The four defendants attended church services at a little frame building named Hopewell Hall about two miles away. Mary Smith claimed to be afraid to go home alone, and the other three walked her home. On the walk back, the four young friends may have conceived the murder plan.

Newspaper accounts describe Mary Piper Smith, 18, as an attractive young girl, and Vesther Ferneau, 23, as a striking brunette. Mary confided to her friend Vesther that she (Mary) was unhappy with her husband and planned to leave him.

The plot thickens as we learn the two young frontier women had befriended the two young bachelors.

Neighbors said Vesther Ferneau's husband, age 46, a hard-drinking riverboat gambler, frequently left his beautiful young wife, age 23, alone on the prairie to tend the farm and care for their four children.

According to early accounts, when the four reached the Smith home, a half-dugout sod house, Mrs. Smith called her husband's name from a distance away as if in distress.

Henry Sam Houston had stationed himself to the side of the house with a heavy wood and metal harness singletree—the murder weapon—in his hand. Edward

Smith opened the door and looked out. He was unable to see anyone in the darkness.

Smith was a tall man and the house had a low doorway. He ducked his head to come outside and at that moment, before regaining his stance, received a blow on the back of his head knocking him unconscious.

The newspaper of the day, under a headline "Foul Murder" reported it this way: "His skull was crushed by the blow and a pool of blood a few feet from the door indicated that he must have fallen without a struggle."

Now realizing the seriousness of their deed and thinking the man was dead, the four tried to make the death look like an accident.

According to the "information" report, White and Houston tied Smith behind his own horse. They caused the horse to drag the body a distance away. As the horse came through the gate, the unconscious man's head caught on a stabilizer wire which broke his neck. They left him in a haystack on a neighboring farm.

The newspaper account read: "The murderers then tied a rope about the dead man's neck and dragged him out into the road and along to a canyon about a half mile from the house. The clothing was dragged off and the surface of the body scratched and cut in a horrible manner."

A coroner's jury was called at Woodward to determine cause of death. All four suspects appeared in court on December 5, 1906. Four months later in April 1907, murder charges were filed in Woodward County against Sam Houston and Vesther Ferneau.

The next month, the grand jury indicted Sam Houston for murder but later dismissed the charge and released the suspect.

On October 19, 1907, they released Vesther Ferneau after eight months in jail on $5,000 bail, no doubt posted by her husband.

Mary Smith and Harrison White, also charged with the murder, were later released as well. Apparently, they turned state's evidence and gained release on condition they testify against their cohorts.

Each defendant's "application for bail" makes pretty much the same statement; they were framed, and they don't know anything about this murder.

At trial the jury found Sam Houston and Mrs. Ferneau not guilty and released them. Mary Smith and Harrison White had already been released.

The murder of Edward "Scotty" Smith went unpunished forever.

WOODWARD BULLETIN
Friday June 5, 1908
"No conviction in the Smith murder case. The parties charged with the crime are free. The case against White, Smith, Ferneau, and Houston ended after three and a half days in district court this week. White and Smith were dismissed as state's witnesses. County Attorney Willett for the state, Swindall and Hoover served for defense."

Two weeks later, the WOODWARD BULLETIN account continued:
"Justice halted—or better, stumbled, for county officer's incompetency. The case dragged through several terms of court. The belief was general that one or all four were guilty but with his usual incompetence the county attorney blundered.

"Strangely enough after murder charges were dropped, the widow Mary Piper Smith, by then 20 years old, married her arresting officer and jailer, Edmund A. "Ash" Smith, age 35, who had almost the same name as her dead husband."

Ash and Mary Smith farmed and operated a music store, never had children, and quietly lived out their lives in Woodward County.

Vesther Ferneau and her husband divorced and moved away. Ash Smith died in 1935 and is buried in the Woodward cemetery. Although some family members still believe Mary poisoned her second husband, no further record is found of her nor of the two bachelors, Sam Houston and Harrison White.

Only that rough white fieldstone in the prairie grass remains as a reminder of the murder and marks the grave of the victim "Scotty" Smith.

Although no headstone carries his name or vital record information, he is still remembered by the old-timers a century later although his murderer remains unpunished.

Parting Shots

An inscription on a tombstone or monument commemorating a dead person or in memory of the person buried there is known as an epitaph. Some phrases penned in memory of a deceased person display a sense of humor, such as this one on a grave from the 1880s in Nantucket, Massachusetts:

> *Under the sod and under the trees*
> *Lies the body of Jonathan Pease.*
> *He is not here, there's only the pod.*
> *Pease shelled out and went to God.*

My own favorite epitaph is this often-quoted one, said to have been found in a cemetery in England:

> *Remember man, as you walk by,*
> *As you are now, so once was I*
> *As I am now, so shall you be.*
> *Remember this and follow me.*

That epitaph is not at all funny, until someone added this postscript:
> *To follow you I'll not consent*
> *Until I know which way you went.*

Masks of deceased persons once a tradition in many countries, have become quite rare. See Figure #97. Before the widespread availability of photography, creating death masks sometimes preserved facial features of unidentified bodies, so that relatives of the deceased could identify them.

Figure 45: A death mask.

Figure 46: Guard dog in Kentucky cemetery.

We found an unusual dog tombstone (Figure 98) in Frankfort, Kentucky, near the grave of Daniel Boone. Perhaps he guards his master's grave, or maybe the master wanted to pay a tribute to his deceased pet.

Figure 47: Death's Head or Soul Effigy tombstones were popular in New England.

These grinning skulls from the 1600s evolved into cherub-like faces with angel wings in the 1800s. This one is from a Connecticut graveyard. The winged skull most often is seen as a dead person's journey when they are flying away to another realm. In the United States, the 'death's head' was initially a non-religious symbol simply used to denote a buried corpse, as the Puritans didn't believe in using religious symbols on graves.

In Summary:

- ✓ Many older graves are marked with flat fieldstones.
- ✓ Each symbol on the tombstone has a hidden meaning.
- ✓ Stones may be marked with affiliation to organizations that may hold more info for you.
- ✓ Gravestones tell a story of the person's life and interests.
- ✓ Cemeteries are really open-air museums displaying fine works of sculpture.

Figure 48: The Weeping Angel of Athens, OH.

CHAPTER THIRTEEN

Genealogy Programs

Computers make genealogy much easier.

You can start with a pencil and paper, but if you really want to make headway—and have more fun—you need a computer.

Genealogy Software Programs are everywhere. When choosing your program be sure it meets these requirements: easy to use, easy to understand, easy to document sources and that it provides links from the source to the information for footnotes. Choose it carefully because once you have your program set up and start filling it in, the challenge to start over with a different program is too overwhelming.

Most genealogy programs work on only Macintosh (Apple) or Windows (Microsoft) computers. Perhaps there is a program that will work on both operating systems, but I am not aware of it. When you shop for genealogy software, be sure to read over the requirements section. If it doesn't list your computer type, or your computer operating system, don't buy it because it will not work.

I use a program named Reunion by Leister Productions. Reunion is especially designed for the Macintosh computer. You can learn more about each program in the list below by typing the name of the program into your search browser (such as Google). Most of the Macintosh computers now available use operating system OSX or ten, with regular upgrades available usually at additional cost.

These ten are the top-rated computer programs this year made specifically for the Apple *Macintosh* computer.

- Heredis
- Family Tree Maker
- Roots Magic
- Reunion
- Ancestral Quest
- MacFamilyTree
- Family Tree Builder
- iFamily
- Osk
- GEDit COM

For Computers Other Than Apple...

There are many good, reasonably priced genealogy software programs available for computers other than Macintosh, so many we'd need a separate book to list them all. By the time this book is published another dozen will probably be available. I personally like Legacy Family Tree. I ran it on my husband's laptop computer, which uses a Windows operating system.

The top six genealogy software programs that work on the Windows OS offer a full slate of features yet are designed for beginners. These are:

Legacy Family Tree. Legacy is available as a free download. The free version is the same as the purchased version with fewer bells and whistles. This provides a great way to get started without a bunch of bundled genealogy data. As you feel more comfortable you can upgrade, and information you have already entered will be automatically imported to the full program.

Family Tree Maker, version 2009 or better. This program remains popular and continues to be a top seller. A user manual is available free online.

Generations Family Tree. Reviews say this full-featured genealogy program is a breeze with step-by-step multimedia tutorial and easy-to-read user manual. Several packages are available. Grande Suite 8.5 package appears to offer the best value for beginning researchers with an amazing collection of data CDs, including the entire 1800 U.S. census. Check current online reviews before buying.

Roots Magic. Some say Roots Magic is the easiest-to-use family tree software available for Windows OS yet is also one of the most powerful. It is available on free trial. Created by Bruce Buzbee and endorsed by Dick Eastman of Eastman's Online Genealogy Newsletter. Roots Magic Publisher allows you to create complete books with narrative, notes, charts, photos, source bibliography, index, and much more.

Ancestral Quest is another popular program. Step-by-step tutorials, good source citation capabilities and beautiful printouts are just some of the features.

Personal Ancestral File (PAF), PAF 5.2, popular personal genealogy software from The Church of Jesus Christ of Latter-day Saints (LDS), helps users organize their family history records. This program is available for free download from www.familysearch.org or for $6 on CD-ROM through the church's distribution centers. The PAF Companion 5.0, a utility designed to print a variety of charts and reports from PAF files, is also available for small fee.

Shop and Compare

Type into your browser's search box: "Compare genealogy software" to see how the different programs are rated. Many programs offer a free trial period or a free demo version, so you may want to try out a couple before deciding on your purchase.

Lots of Info to Look for When Using a Computer

As you become more efficient and interested in the search, you may want to investigate other genealogical sources available on the Internet. New databases are being published every day, and books with lists of good database sites become obsolete even before they hit the racks.

The amount of information available online is amazing. Most came about through the Freedom of Information act; however, there is talk of limiting access. Worries about identity theft add to concern.

Information you find on the Internet is only a clue until it is verified. Ancestry.com and other on-line genealogy sites are useful but must be consulted with a high degree of suspicion, especially any family history information entered without sources. Ancestry's World Family Tree can provide clues for you, but quality of the information depends on the accuracy of researchers' submissions, which can be very spotty—the old GIGO (Garbage In, Garbage Out) dilemma.

Who is Cyndi?

Going to Cyndi's List www.cyndislist.com website brings you to Cyndi Howells' home page. Cyndi says when she started her little list of favorite websites, she had no idea it would eventually bring her such fame and fortune.

Scroll down to the **"Personal Home Pages"** category. Then click on the letter of the alphabet for your surname. If you don't find any pages with your family name, even though there must be thousands in there, don't despair. I tried all four of my grandparents' surnames and did not find one that matched—except for my great-grandmother Mary Smith. I saw a plethora of Mary Smith names, but none matched my great-grandmother's profile.

The one name you are looking for may not be obvious. The list is alphabetical by name of the web page, not the family. Try this: Go to the top of Cyndi's page, click on "Search Cyndi's List," and enter the name you want. You should see lots of hits causing you to spend hours having fun investigating all the many leads.

Definitely not a mailing list and not quite a message board, the RootsWeb Surname List <rsl.rootsweb.com> (yes, that is the correct URL) is a registry of last names and people who are researching them. According to the webpage, the list on the day I searched featured almost a million surnames submitted by two hundred thousand genealogists, with additional names arriving at the rate of more than seven hundred a day. Each surname on the list shows dates and locations of interest to the submitter, plus his or her contact information.

There are thousands of personal web sites devoted to surname research and compiling data. You probably have an ancestor on more than one of them.

TRUE STORY: In Danville, Kentucky, there is a whole museum dedicated to the surname "**Jones**."

From their webpage www.thegoldenlionbb.com you learn the museum is located in a bed and breakfast named **The Golden Lion**, a beautiful 1840 Greek revival home listed on the National Register of Historic Places. The Golden Lion provides genealogical resources to those interested in researching the JONES surname.

The home's library, museum, and research center are centered on the private collections of Dr. Jerry Jones, a genealogist who has researched his family name for more than thirty years.

The Golden Lion bed and breakfast is located in historic Danville, Kentucky, the site of the Constitutional Convention bringing Kentucky into the Union as the fifteenth state. The Old Wilderness Road, which runs through Danville, was the major land route used by the early settlers traveling from Virginia to Kentucky. This road is a key genealogical connection for those researching families in Kentucky. If you are a Jones, or are seeking information about a Jones link, the proprietor can describe the origin and development of the surname in Wales beginning around 40AD through the early 1600s. Each bedroom is named for one of the Jones family ancestors.

This is not an endorsement of the B&B because I have not stayed there. I *do* hope to go, even though I do not have a Jones in my ancestry. (update: In 2018, the Jones family decided to close the B&B because of their advancing ages. They donated their collections to nearby museums.)

Surname Studies

The quickest way to find a surname study is to use one of the major search engines such as Google *www.google.com*, AltaVista *www.altavista.com*, or dog pile *www.dogpile.com*. There are others, too. Just put your surname into the search blank and you will probably get hundreds of hits. The top ones listed are usually best.

Check with Cyndi's List for more ideas on searching for Internet information on your family. Remember, some sites are fee-based, and some are free, but most will allow a trial period or at least a search before you invest, that's an easy way to see if they have anything worth your time and money.

Splurge on a Membership

My personal favorite genealogy program is **Ancestry.com,** mentioned previously. You can search their census, military, and other databases for free although you will be asked to sign up for an account to view the record. Sometimes they offer a fourteen-day free trial membership. Other times they offer half-price.

Ancestry.com offers a free online family tree, some always-free databases, and several other options. The basic membership costs above a hundred dollars a year, but you can use it free at most public libraries anytime.

Heritage Quest (HQ) has excellent census searches. If you don't wish to buy a membership, check your local library to see if they have Heritage Quest (HQ) online. Most of the historical society libraries, the LDS (family history) research centers, and even many public libraries offer this program and others. Often you can access the program from your home computer using your library card.

Another great program available at some libraries and most historical research facilities is **Footnote.com**. You can use the Footnote indexes free at your home computer, but the full program comes for an annual membership fee, unless you are at a participating library. The Footnote.com collections feature documents never before available on the Internet, relating to the Revolutionary War, Civil War, WWI, WWII, US Presidents, historical newspapers, naturalization documents, and many more. Millions of pages are already created from public records including the Social Security Death Index and WWII Army Enlistment Records. Members of Footnote have created thousands of pages on their own using information found on Vietnam and USS Arizona memorials, 1860 and 1930 Census, or other images.

Familysearch.org, a service of the Church of Jesus Christ of Latter-Day Saints (LDS), the program is free and can be accessed from your home computer. Type your ancestor's name into the website search box and you may be pleasantly surprised by what information pops up.

Many other databases are available and new ones seem to appear every day.

In Summary

- ✓ Genealogy software programs for computers are plentiful, some work on both types of computer platforms.
- ✓ There are two main types of computers—Apple and the Others. My biased opinion may be showing here.
- ✓ Some programs offer a trial period to help you choose.
- ✓ Search engines can help you find others researching your family name.

CHAPTER FOURTEEN

Courthouse Treasures

See you in court!

You gotta' go to the courthouses to meet three important people—the County Clerk, the Court Clerk and the County Treasurer

Local court records are not the first place you want to begin searching, but it is fun to plan a trip to the county where your ancestors lived. I have done it many times and always come away with new friends and a new outlook on what life was like in earlier days. One never knows what will turn up at the courthouse.

Be sure to plan your trip wisely and carefully. Before you go, create a checklist with names, dates, and details for each record you plan to research in advance of your visit, and then check them off as you go. By focusing your search on just a few ancestors or a few record types, you'll be more likely to achieve your research goals. If you are not familiar with courthouses, the first thing you need to learn is the difference between Court Clerk records and County Clerk records. Big difference.

Check the *Handy Book for Genealogists* to learn about the county you want to search. Last published in 2006, the 11th edition is the most current and can be purchased from Ebay. *The Handy Book,* as it is commonly called, is a guide to chronology and development of counties in each state, listing for each county the date created, parent county, county seat and federal censuses available, and more. This book presents one of the most valuable bibliography collections available to genealogists.

The Eleventh edition of the *Handy Book for Genealogists* integrates the winning formula of previous editions with a number of new features. The genius of this book is its capacity to provide the researcher with at-a-glance genealogical guidance for every county in the U.S. The book is now out-of-print but used copies can often be found online as cheap as a couple bucks plus shipping.

Counties Have Ancestors Too!

County lines often changed, new counties were carved out of old ones, and some counties disappeared. The records of your ancestors should be found in the counties as they were when your ancestors lived there. If the county line changed, the records up to that date should be in the original county. You will need to visit the county seat—the administrative center for the county you want to search. That is where you will find the courthouse. The county seat town is not necessarily the largest town, and some counties even have two courthouses. If your ancestors lived near a county line, you may find them documented among the records of the adjoining county. The *Handy Book* can guide you on where you need to go.

If your ancestors lived in the U.S. before the late 1800s, their names are likely to be in the minute books or other records of the county courts. That office handled not only minor criminal matters, but also small lawsuits and a vast range of legal papers and administrative duties that touched the lives of nearly everyone. As a lawyer friend said, "In the beginning the Constitution created the county courts, and they handled everything important to the people."

How Many Courts in one Courthouse?

Now there are District Courts, Circuit Courts, Appellate Courts, and many others, in addition to the state and federal court system. That is too complicated to explain here. This chapter is about the County Courts—different in every county of every state.

Counties have ancestors too! County lines often changed, new counties were carved out of old ones, and some counties disappeared. The records are in the counties as they were when your ancestors lived there.

When Is the Best Time to Go?

Even if the *Handy Book* gives the hours an office is open, call first (the phone number is in the *Handy Book*). Ask that office if any certain time is better for your visit. Each state and each county seem to have their own system, so you need to know before you go which office actually has the records you are seeking.

Plan to arrive early in the day and check in with the clerk of the office you want to visit. Do not take up the county official's time with unnecessary chatter. They are not interested in your family history. All county offices seem to be understaffed and underpaid; many clerks think genealogists are time wasters. In most county courthouses, office hours are 8:30 to 4:30, and they usually ask everyone to leave by 4:00 so they can get their desks cleaned off and shut down for the day.

What to Take

Courthouse offices are often small and cramped, so it is best to keep your take-along to a minimum. You need only a notepad, pencils, coins for the photocopier and parking, your research checklist with names, dates, and details for each record you plan to research, a Family History Sheet or brief summary of what you already know about the family, and a digital camera. If you plan to take a laptop computer, charge your battery before you go, because electrical access probably won't be available. Keep in mind that some facilities will not permit cameras or laptops.

Take your list of what you want to find, with vital information and dates. Bring several dollar bills and a roll or two of quarters and dimes to feed the copy machine. You never know until you get there what you will need to do to get copies of records. At one courthouse I visited recently, the only copies I was allowed to make were by taking a picture with my cellphone.

Be extra polite if you want those clerks to help you at all.

TRUE STORY: In Indiana we performed all the preliminary niceties. When we showed up to copy one document, the workers were enjoying birthday cake in the records room and had posted a closed sign on the door. Luckily, I had a "cousin" with me who lived in that county. He sweet-talked the clerk into letting us move the cake off the copier, so we were able to make the copy we needed and go on our way.

The Dressing Dilemma—What to Wear

Dress professionally. The clerks will treat you better if you do not look like a homeless bum coming inside to get warm. Casual dressy is the term that seems to fit. A sport coat for men unless it is very warm weather, and a nice slacks suit for ladies is appropriate.

Wear flat, comfortable shoes because courthouses and annexes are usually very old buildings with uneven floors. You may need to climb several flights of stairs, which can be narrow and steep. You will need to climb a ladder to reach the heavy, bound books. If you are unable to do that, bring someone with you who can. The clerks cannot take the time to get the books down for you.

Do Your Work Before You Go

You need to review what you want to find and which office at the courthouse should have the particular paper you are looking for. Once there, the choices on where to begin may be a little overwhelming.

- Marriage records are usually in the court clerk's office.
- Death records—such as wills, probate, estate—probably will be filed in the court clerk's office; sometimes they are in the recorder's office.
- Civil & criminal cases should be in record books of the court clerk.
- Citizenship & Naturalization records are probably found in the court clerk records.
- Land records should be in the <u>county</u> clerk's office or with the registrar of deeds.
- Military records are probably in the county clerk's office.
- Tax records will be filed in the county treasurer's office.

But not always.

Different counties do it differently.

You can always ask at the courthouse where to find the records you are looking for, but it usually works better to research before you leave home. Once you have that information and know where you want to go and what you hope to find, you are ready to pack your suitcase, gas up the Ford, and hit the road.

Start in the County Clerk's Office

For information about land ownership, go to the county clerk's office. The record you seek may be across the hall or down the street in a county recorder's office but start with the clerk. Deeds are almost always well indexed and cared for, because land ownership has always been important. Land was the symbol of power, wealth, and social status in the Old World. Immigrants took countless risks coming to the New Country to acquire land.

By law, county commissioners in each county are responsible for maintaining these records, and in most places they turn that responsibility over to their clerk. (Be particularly nice to this person!) **Note:** some states do not have county commissioners, but if not, there will be an equivalent office to maintain real estate ownership records.

Land records include deeds, mortgages, land warrants, liens, sheriff sales, survey books, entry books, commissioners' deed books.

Know what you need and know the time period you are looking for. Because you have done your homework, you can confidently tell the county clerk, for example, *"I want to see the deed indexes for 1800 to 1875 (or whatever years you need)."*

Deeds

Deeds are the bulk and backbone of American land records. Before land could be privately owned the government had to pass title into private hands. In most cases in the U.S., the authorities "bought" title from the local Indian tribes, although the Indians did not really understand the concept of ownership.

Figure 49: A county clerk's office record room.

This county clerk's office in Harper County, Oklahoma, is well organized and neatly arranged. Not all offices are like this.

The government offered the land to settlers as a grant or patent for homesteading. For every tract of land there should be a first-title deed, normally called a grant or patent. Many older deed records and indexes have been archived and moved from the county courthouse to another building.

There are several types of early deeds, but two are most common. One is the **transfer of ownership** of land and buildings. Before 1865, you may even find transfer of ownership of slaves.

The other type is a **deed of trust**, which might be written for various circumstances. A man in debt in the nineteenth century often gave a deed of trust to pay off his creditors or to release a mortgage. He gave the deed to a friend or relative for a dollar or two. If he could not pay off his debt, then the trustee was authorized to sell the property and use the money to pay the debt.

For transfer of ownership of land, the seller (grantor) signed a deed and gave it to the buyer (grantee) in exchange for money as proof of the sale. The buyer was responsible for having the deed recorded at the courthouse. The deed may have remained with the clerk a few days until it was transcribed into a deed book, and then the new owner was expected to come back to claim the original.

Some buyers forgot to retrieve the original paper, and a hundred years later you might find it still in the folder. Forgetting or neglecting to pick up the original deed apparently happened a lot in Wayne County, Illinois, as evidenced in the following newspaper story. Of course, the original papers are gone forever now since the courthouse burned in the late 1800s. I wonder how they were able to reconstruct those land records.

TRUE STORY: (*Wayne Co Enterprise, November 8, 1886*) "There was [sic] probably over 1,000 deeds in the Circuit Clerk's offices which had been recorded but which had not been called for. Such carelessness will now cost the owners of the land considerable expenses in many cases."

Who is the Grantee?

Deed books are usually indexed in separate volumes by the names *Grantee Index* (buyers) and *Grantor Index* (sellers). You should check both lists and write down the volume and page number for each one you want to read.

Perhaps at the top of your priority list is your desire to examine the deed to the old family farm—didn't every family have one in the 1800s and 1900s? Land records offer the most valuable genealogical records, often naming children and grandchildren.

Land transfers were not always recorded at the time ownership transferred.

If the farm went to a child by inheritance, you may not find any record until it is sold to someone outside the family. Often deeds were exchanged within the family and never recorded, to save paying the recording fee. Some were not recorded until years later, so be sure to save the date of recording as well as the date of the deed.

Deeds are always indexed under both seller and buyer. There might be separate index books for each, or they might be listed together in one book called a *General Index* or *Grantor-Grantee Index*.

Open the index book and study the inside front cover. You should find a diagram or chart with an explanation of the indexing system used in that county. Read it carefully, because there are many variations.

Types of Land Ownership Transfers

Once you understand the index and determine how to use it, look for entries that name your family. The entry should include the name of both grantor and grantee, the date of the document, and the date recorded, the type of document and the book and page where the action is recorded. It may also give a very short property description. Copy all this information.

You can't transfer real estate without having something in writing, which is almost always some type of deed. This document transfers ownership of real estate and contains the names of the old and new owners, a legal description of the property, and is signed by the person transferring the property.

Pay particular attention to the type of document. Typical descriptions are warranty deed, deed of trust, gift deed, power of attorney, petition of partition—and there may only be an acronym for the type such as WD for warranty deed. Each is a different way of conveying title or ownership of property, and it is important to know the difference.

Acronyms are Important

The county record books usually show acronyms. The following are the most common.

QCD -A quitclaim deed transfers whatever ownership interest a person has in a property with no guarantee about the extent of the person's interest. Divorcing couples commonly use quitclaim deeds where one spouse signs all his or her rights in the couple's real estate over to the other. Quitclaim can be especially useful if it isn't clear how much of an interest, if any, one spouse has in property that is held in the other's name. However, a quitclaim deed doesn't relieve the individual transferring ownership from responsibility for the mortgage, if there is one. Quitclaim deeds are also frequently used when there is a "cloud" on the title—that is, when a search reveals a previous owner or some other individual, like the heir of a previous owner, may have some claim to the property.

GRD -A grant deed transfers ownership and implies a promise that the title hasn't already been transferred to someone else or been encumbered in any way, except as set out in the deed.

WD -A warranty deed transfers ownership and explicitly promises the buyer that the person making the transfer has good title to the property, meaning it is free of liens or claims of ownership. The grantor guarantees he or she will compensate the buyer if that turns out to be wrong. The warranty deed may make other promises as well, to address particular problems with the transaction.

BSD -A bargain and sale deed implies the grantor has the right to convey title but makes no warranties against encumbrances. This type of deed is most commonly used by court officials or fiduciaries that hold the property by force of law rather than title, such as properties seized for unpaid taxes and sold at sheriff's sale. You will need this information in your next step to find the document.

The deed record books are usually stored in a fireproof vault, and if you are lucky the clerk will show you into the vault. From there you are on your own, and there is more to that story. Some old records are maintained in good condition; many have even been rebound, and a few have been laminated. However, you may find yourself relegated instead to a dark, dusty basement with the books thrown in a corner in no order at all. Good luck.

What Book to Choose First

Think of the County Clerk's office as a library. The books are usually marked on their spines with the type of record the volume contains. Look for the book labeled "Deeds." Numbering systems vary from one office to another. If the earliest deed books start with A, B, C, the next set may begin with 1, 2, 3—or some other method.

You may remove a book from the shelf and put it on the counter for examination but be certain to put it back where you got it when you are finished. Other researchers will be working on the same counter so courteously use as little counter space as possible.

One thing I was slow to learn; the signatures in the deed books are **not** the original signatures of your ancestors. The clerk copied the deed and the signature from the original. Sometimes he/she may have even tried to duplicate the appearance of the signature. If the person signed with an X or a *hand mark*, the clerk often tried to picture that mark as it was drawn on the deed.

Hand Mark Signatures

Some ancestors in early days created elaborate "hand marks," a type of signature similar to a cattle brand, when they were unable to write. Hand marks range from a very simple X to a stylized letter, often the first letter of the first or last name of the individual, to very elaborate designs. Some individuals probably just drew some lines, added a loop here and a swirl there, and that became their hand mark.

Others probably created a symbol with meaning for them. Perhaps it represented where they lived, their status, occupation, or a physical characteristic. You will want to make a copy of any hand mark.

Be sure to make a note of the book or volume and page you find for an ancestor.

If a person signed his name to some documents and later signs his will or deeds with a mark, the change might suggest blindness or other infirmity rather than lack of schooling.

What do you do when you find one?

As stated earlier, deeds are universally indexed under both seller (grantor) and buyer (grantee), but every county keeps these records by its own method. A clerk might suggest that you need only look at the grantee index, and not the grantor, saying if there is no record a person bought land, there could be no record of selling it. Don't listen to that.

There could be many reasons why the transfer was not entered so always check both indexes. Again, you do have to open the index book and see if there is a diagram or chart explaining the particular index system used in that county.

Once you find your family name in the index, copy all the entries for that purchase or sale. Sometimes a cooperative county clerk will allow you to use their copier, sometimes not. I take along a digital camera for those times. Other people may carry portable scanners.

Once you find what you are looking for in the index, begin your search for the recorded deed, which may have the family information you need. Using the data you copied from the index you should locate the right deed book. Carefully pull that book out from the shelf and place it on the counter to examine it.

When you do find the deed you want, you can either transcribe it or get it copied. Using a Deed Transcript Form (DTF) facilitates the work. The DTF form is downloadable from the companion website to this book: www.whosyourdaddybook.com.

I always make a copy if the deed requires only a page or two, but the costs can mount up quickly, at least a dollar or more a page. The clerks may prefer to do the copying themselves or they may direct you to a copier. When you finish with the record book, be sure to put it back exactly where you found it.

You may not have time this trip to look up each record, but you will have your data list ready when you come back. Be certain you copied names of both buyer and seller, date, type of document, book and page. If you are unable to return to the courthouse, you may be able to use that information to find the record you need at your local LDS Family History Library. The LDS microfilmed most of the early courthouse records.

Oh, Those Lovely Court Records

For information about estates, lawsuits, marriages, divorces, guardianships, go to the clerk of the COURT.

A few generations ago, citizens attended their local court proceedings as a civic duty. To be honest, it was their main social function and they were happy to be there. Every three months or so during court week, the county courthouse buzzed with activity as people studied the cases on the docket and gossiped about them. While there they cook care of other business, registering deeds, probating wills, paying taxes, applying for a business license, complaining about a quarrelsome neighbor, discussing upkeep of roads and bridges, flirting with potential mates, contracting marriages—it all happened on court week.

Up to the time of the Civil War, county criminal prosecutions might include a scolding wife or a gossip, witchcraft, someone disrespectful to the minister, a person who broke the "blue laws" by keeping a business open on Sunday, or someone refusing to attend church.

The older records may be in another office, an annex, or even another building. There is usually a directory at the courthouse entrance.

Wills, Estates and Probates

Estates: There are two kinds of estates: **testate** (with a will) and **intestate** (without a will). If the person owned real or personal property, an estate was filed in the county of residence. Note: Some people did not have sufficient property to require a court proceeding.

Probates: Probate to prove and administer a will has another process. An executor or administrator is appointed, and notice given when the will shall be heard, so anyone who wants to contest the will can appear. After the probate is approved, the clerk transcribes the will into a will book, assigning a book and page number. The probate packets can be quite lengthy and are full of useful information.

Probate records are among the earliest records available and help document family relationships. These will be found in the courthouse of the county where the deceased lived at the time of death. Probates are usually filed in the court clerk's office or equivalent office by some other name. The official in charge of probate records may be called clerk of probate court, register of probate, county court clerk, clerk of orphan's court, clerk of surrogate court, clerk of the ordinary—or something else.

A will may list the spouse, all the children by their given names, grandchildren by name, married names of daughters, even their husband's names and where they live, and other family members. But you cannot count on it. You may instead find the will refers only to "my beloved wife" and "all my children" without naming any of them.

Usually included are papers detailing settlement of the **estate**, and these may show who inherited the family home. Records may include the will, an inventory, and other papers. Sometimes each knife and fork, every head of livestock, books in the bookcase, every piece of furniture, tablecloths, dishes, quilts, and tools were counted and recorded. In the report of sale, you may learn who bought each item and how much they paid. This gives you a picture of the lifestyle or financial status of the family. On one inventory and sale in early Kentucky, the widow had to buy back her own pots and pans from the estate.

Be sure to note the file number, book and page numbers, and the date of probate. Ask for a copy of the will and other estate papers for your source files.

If your ancestor owned property in another county, you should check the court records there also. Wills are not always filed immediately, so search beyond dates of the person's death. If a wife is named, do not assume she is the mother of all the children named in the will. Remember too, terms in early records that imply relationships such as sister, cousin, brother, etc., may not mean what you think.

Perhaps a minor inherited some property and the court appointed a guardian to manage his or her estate until the "age of majority." To reach the age of majority means to come of legal age, usually age 21 for males and 18 for females. The age of majority differed from state to state in different time periods.

Guardianships

The court appointed guardians for minor children for two main reasons.
- ✓ Either one or both parents were deceased, or
- ✓ The minor child was named as an heir in a grandparent's estate. The father of the child was usually named guardian.

In guardianship records you may find that when a man died, even though his wife was living, a guardian had to be appointed for the children. However, if the mother died and the father was living, no guardian was needed.

Minor children over age fourteen were allowed to choose their guardians. The court appointed guardians for younger children. Sometimes guardians were required to post a bond, and in some instances, you may find an inventory or account of how the children's expenses for clothes and schooling were paid. A final accounting occurred when the minor reached age 21, so you can determine age from that record. The Court also appointed adult guardians when needed.

TRUE STORY: Elizabeth Williams Stribling was the daughter of a minister and later became wife of a minister, but when her husband, the Rev. George W. Stribling, died ca 1848-1850, the $100 had to be posted to be sure the mother took care of the six youngsters. It must have been very difficult for Elizabeth to come up with $100 back then when preachers were poor as church mice.

She remarried three months later.

Names of witnesses on legal papers are an important factor, as there is almost always a familial relationship. Witnesses on this guardianship were Benjamin W. Williams, who turned out to be Elizabeth's brother, and Hamilton Farthing, a close neighbor. The date of this guardianship is August 1851.

We have been unable to learn a date of death for George Stribling, but the 1850 census, taken June 1, lists Elizabeth Stribling as a widow. Rev. Stribling had to have been dead for a year or more by the time of the guardianship appointment so we can estimate his death about 1848.

NOTE: Name is shown on the court document spelled as pronounced Striblin, without a terminal "g." Absence of punctuation makes transcribing the old handwriting even more difficult.

Guardianship Bond Transcription

Know all men by these presents: That we: Elizabeth Striblin, Hamilton Farthing, and Benjamin W. Williams of the county of Marion and state of Illinois are held and firmly bound unto the people of the state of Illinois in the penal sum of one hundred dollars for the use of Mary Ann, Bradford S., Margaret E., Sarah M., and Mahala C. Striblin minor heirs of George Striblin deceased for the payment of which well and truly to be

made we bind ourselves, our heirs, executors and administrators, jointly, severally and firmly by these presents.
Witness, our hands and our seal,
this 6th day of August AD 1851.

Sample Guardianship Bond and Transcription

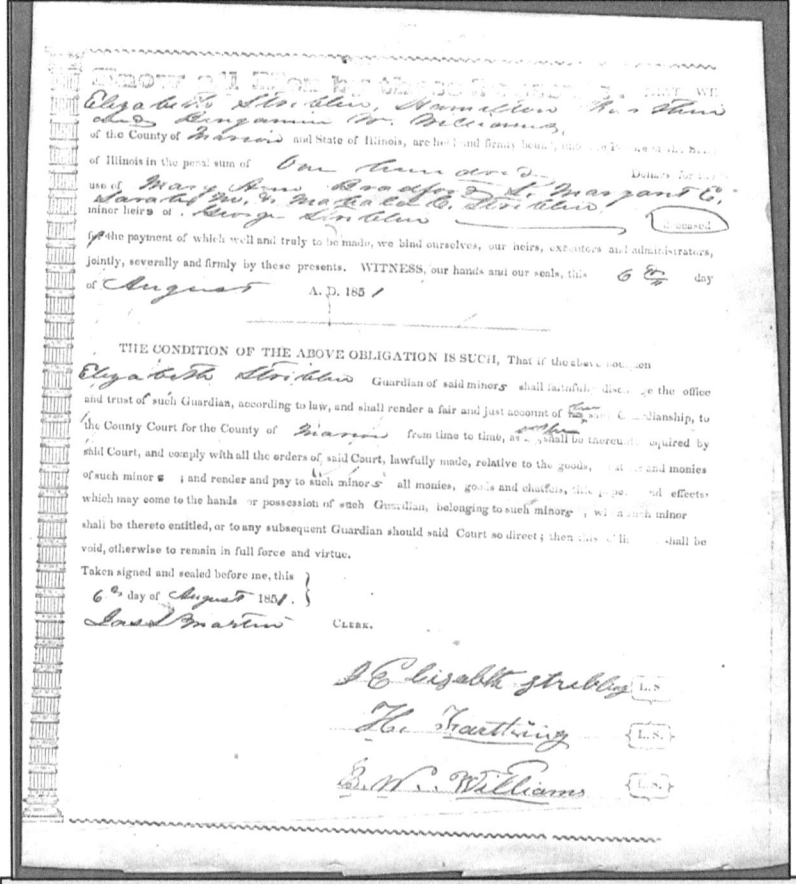

Figure 50: Guardianship of Elizabeth (Williams) Stribling's children, probate court records, Marion County, Illinois, 1851.

The condition of the above obligation is such, that if the above bounden Elizabeth Striblin, guardian of said minors shall faithfully discharge the office and trust of such Guardian, according to law, and shall render a fair and just account of her said Guardianship, to the County Court for the County of Marion from time to time, as she shall be thereunto required by said Court, and comply with all the orders of said Court, lawfully made, relative to the goods, chattels and monies of such minors and render and pay to such minors all monies, goods and chattels, title papers and effects, which may come to the hands or possession of such Guardian, belonging to such minors, when such minor shall be thereto entitled or to any subsequent Guardian should said Court so direct; then this obligation shall be void, otherwise to remain in full force and virtue.

    Taken signed and sealed before me this
6th day of August 1851
Jas. L Martin, Clerk
Signed: Elizabeth Stribling
H. Farthing
B.W. Williams

Sample Marriage Bond and Transcription

Another example of the lack of women's rights at the time of 1851, is that a girl's guardian or her father could bind her in marriage, with the husband-to-be providing a bond to the court.

Marriage bonds, licenses, and intentions are **not** evidence that marriage occurred, only that a marriage was planned.

Till Death (or Divorce) Us Do Part

Usually the marriage and divorce indexes are located in the same office with the estates, but not always.

Everything on the marriage record is significant. You may find the bride's father's name, or her brother's name, or that of a guardian. A couple wishing to be married went to the county clerk with proof of eligibility of marriage—being of legal age and single status. In early days, the groom had to provide bond money as security to guarantee there was no legal or moral reason to prevent the marriage and to affirm he would not back out of the marriage. If he did, he forfeited the money. The bondsman might be a parent, but often a brother or uncle to the bride signed as surety.

To avoid posting bond money, the groom might announce marriage banns. Sometimes a couple was required to do both. Normally these banns were publicly announced for three weeks, usually in church, so that if anyone knew of a reason why one of the partners might be ineligible for marriage, then known facts were announced and no marriage occurred.

If no obstacle appeared the clerk issued a license that was taken by the couple to their minister or a civil authority.

After the marriage was performed, the authority sent a "return" to the clerk, signifying that the marriage had taken place, and the clerk recorded the marriage date. However, the bonds and licenses were also recorded at the time of issue or acceptance, thus the presence of a bond and/or license does not always mean a marriage occurred.

Sometimes the minister or other authority neglected to send a return, or it was subsequently lost, so the marriage was never recorded at the courthouse.

Transcription of 1850 KY marriage bond

Know all men by these presents that we, Geo A. Cozine & Floyd N. Gritton, are held and firmly bound unto the commonwealth of Kentucky in the penal sum of fifty pounds current money to the payment of which well and truly to be made, we bind ourselves, our heirs, and jointly and severally firmly by these presents sealed with our seals and dated this 15 day of Nov. 1851. day of Nov 1851.

The condition of the above obligation is such that whereas there is a license about to issue for a marriage intended to be solemnized between the above bound Geo & Mary Craig.
Now if there be no lawful cause to obstruct said marriage then this obligation to be void else to remain in full force and virtue.

Witness
Tho Allin CC
(signed George A. Cozine (seal)

F. N. Gritton (seal)
[on the back of the certificate, F. N. Gritton made oath "that the within-named Mary Craig is 21 years of age."]

Why did the Groom have to post a Financial Bond?

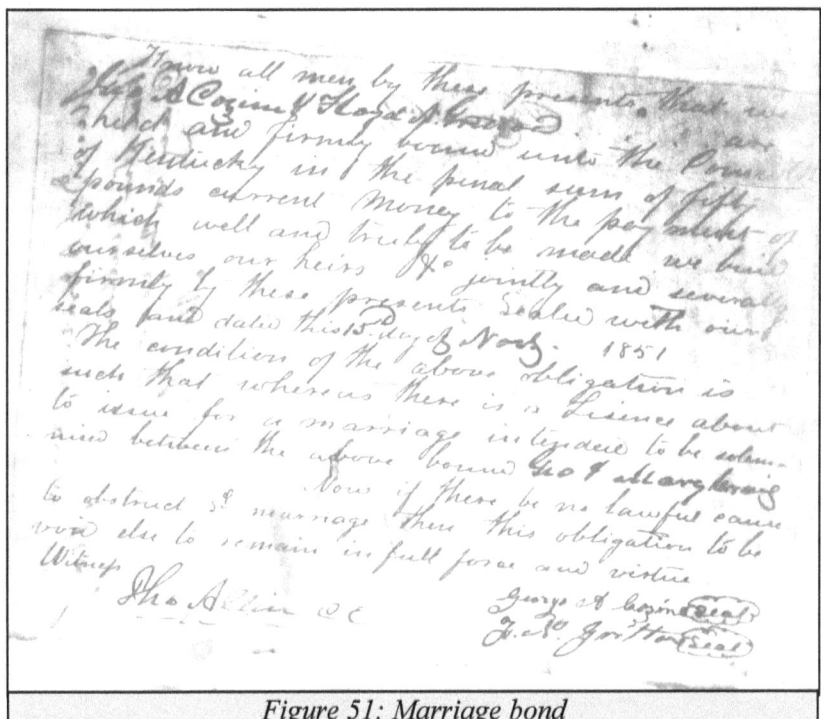

Figure 51: Marriage bond of Mary Craig to George Cozine in Mercer County, Kentucky, 1851.

Other Court Records

Court records cover a wide range of topics, including marriage, divorce, adoption, taxes, naturalization, wills, record of probate (which names the heirs and their addresses), and lawsuits.

Other records you may find in the Court Clerk's office include:

- Guardianships,
- Powers of attorney,
- Tax records,
- Voting records,
- Naturalization records,
- Homestead records,
- Passport applications,
- and a book called:
- Orphans, Apprentices, and the Poor.

Since court records cover such a wide variety of subjects, they can help you in many different ways. For example, they may help you locate ancestors' residences, determine occupations, find financial information, establish citizenship status, or clarify relationships between people. It all depends on the type of court records available where your ancestral names appear.

Naturalization, a voluntary act, is the process by which an alien becomes an American citizen. While aliens often went through the process in district court, they could become naturalized citizens through any court of record, such as a city or county court. We located my German ancestor's 1852 naturalization in probate court records in Ross County, Ohio. Naturalization petitions before 1906 have very little genealogical information.

Where the action is!

County courts were also called "quarter sessions" because they met quarterly. These sessions had criminal jurisdiction in cases that did not involve punishment by death and involved less than a certain amount of money. Older court records are usually the easiest to find, because many have been transferred to a state archive or state library, microfilmed or published.

Three courts.

There are three main types of legal actions in a court of law: Civil, Criminal, and Equity

Civil court actions (person vs. person) involve something one person did to another, that person's property or the reputation of another. The most common civil actions are about property damage, trespass, libel, assault, negligence, etc. Every civil case process starts by issuing a writ of summons, which is a command to appear before the court. The sheriff usually serves the writ on the defendant. Next the plaintiff files a claim or petition to explain why he/she took action. The defendant then files an answer, which is filed with the court clerk. Then it is ready for trial and scheduled on the court's docket. Most jurisdictions encourage the two parties to save money and time and settle out of court.

In Mercer County, Kentucky, once the people were no longer fighting Indian attacks, the court records filled up with civil cases. With no real enemy or danger, the early settlers apparently needed an outlet for energy.

Civil court hears many different kinds of cases. Because civil court cases are not about breaking a criminal law, you might find some great family history information in civil court cases.
- Cases about contracts, damage to property, or someone getting hurt.
- Divorce, child support, and child custody cases.
- Cases about child abuse and neglect or juvenile delinquency.
- Landlord/Tenant conflicts.
- Probate, including wills, trusts, guardianship, conservatorship, name changes, adoption, lunacy, and elder abuse—and sometimes naturalization.
- Small Claims cases—amounts varied by year and by state, but here is a rule of thumb:
- Individual: $7,500 or less
- Business: under $5,000

Criminal court actions (state or people vs. person) involve protection of society. Criminal offenses include felonies such as murder, robbery, burglary, and rape. It also covers misdemeanors such as petty theft, vagrancy, drunkenness, prostitution and breaking the Sabbath. You may hope you don't find any information on your family in this ledger, but those skeletons in the closet add spice to the family history.

In criminal cases you should look for affidavits, charges, lists of evidence, a transcript of the trial, and jury lists. Not all trial transcripts were produced in hard copy. My understanding is someone had to pay for a transcript, or the judge had to order it otherwise none would be made. Here is a digest version of the procedure.

The court orders an offender to appear, usually by issuing a warrant for arrest, and an officer takes the person into custody and usually puts the offender in jail. The accused will have a hearing within a short time so the court can determine if there is enough evidence that a crime was committed and if the accused should be kept in jail until trial.

In the case of murder, the coroner holds an inquest before a jury. The jury gives a verdict about the cause of death. The next step is for the defendant to either plead guilty and be sentenced without a trial or plead not guilty and be "bound over" for trial. If a trial is set, a court representative interviews witnesses and takes depositions from those unable to appear in person.

A jury is drawn from tax rolls, the case is presented by the district attorney and by the defendant's attorney, testimony is heard, written depositions are presented, the attorneys present their summations, and the jury is instructed on the points of law. The judge makes his judgment of punishment based on the jury's verdict.

In early days, verdict and judgment came on the same day. Now the judge's decision may take up to ninety days.

Before 1865, a jail sentence was unusual. Instead of doing time, the convicted person might be publicly whipped, dunked in cold water, sentenced to forced labor, or ordered to pay a fine. Capital crimes were punished by death or banishment.

Each step of a trial generates lots of paper records.

Equity court actions are usually about property rights. Probate, divorce, and adoption are equity actions. Few jurisdictions have three separate courts; one judicial body usually handles all three, although the court minutes may state specifically which hat the judge is wearing for that case.

What If It Is a Burned County?

Many courthouses were destroyed during the Civil War. Others simply caught fire at a time when there was little firefighting equipment, and they burned to the ground. If the clerk tells you the courthouse burned, don't give up.

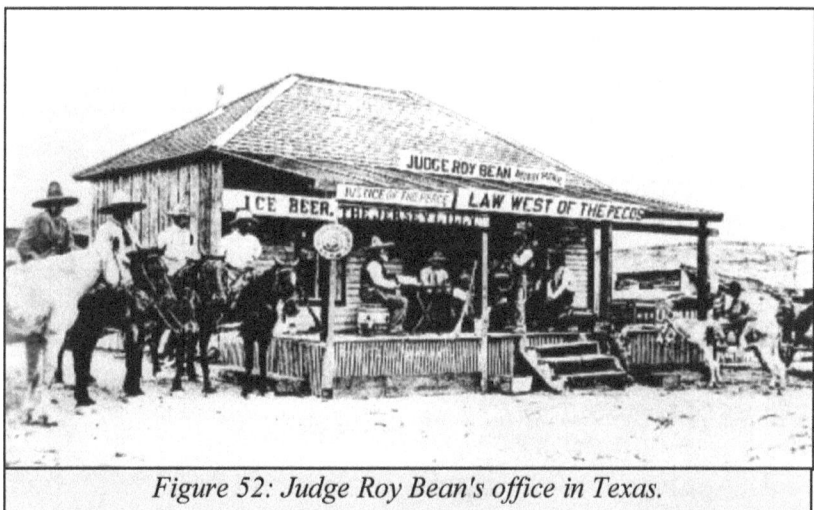

Figure 52: Judge Roy Bean's office in Texas.

Judge Roy Bean (1825-1903), was known as "the hanging judge" even though there was no evidence he ever hanged anyone. Judge Bean held court sessions in his saloon along the Rio Grande River in Pecos County of West Texas.

TRUE STORY: Several years ago, I called the Wayne County, Illinois, courthouse to ask about coming for a visit. The clerk told me the courthouse burned and there were no records prior to 1886. We cancelled the trip.

Many years later I decided to visit the courthouse anyway. That is how I learned that **not all** the records burned. Sadly, deeds and land records did not survive, but we found my great-great-grandfather's will, dated 1862, containing the legal description of his farm. With that information the local library directed us to a history of the church he founded in 1852, listing the names of all his children.

Some courthouses carefully preserved their records, flattening original papers and placing them in file folders. When we visited the Montgomery County Courthouse in Christiansburg, Virginia, we found records from 1773 carefully placed in clear envelopes and filed in three-ring binders by date. The staff was helpful and friendly and their recordkeeping excellent.

Others have done little to preserve records, so they may be in terrible condition. Be prepared for lots of dust, even in the best of conditions.

Taxes and Other Records

Stop by the county treasurer's office to look at the tax records. These papers help you determine what part of the county the family lived in, identify taxable property they owned such as land, horses, cattle, and even personal items, or find a date when they moved in or out of the county.

In early times taxed items include watches, carriages, windows, whiskey, land, and slaves. Tax records are not usually indexed but can often be worth the time it takes to go through them. Names are often listed by the alphabetical letter—by that I mean all the As were together but not further alphabetized.

One man, Arthur Weaner, published a book on the *Taxables of York Co, Pennsylvania in the 1700s* that made it possible to distinguish between three men of the same name. That made it possible to qualify descendants for a lineage society, so tax records can be very important.

You might ask if there are any voting records or early deed abstracts. Many counties published an early county atlas listing landowners by name. In Illinois, we stopped in the county surveyor's office to pick up a county map. He showed us an early map with our ancestor's name and the location of his 1870 plot of land.

If you learn what school your family attended, and if it is still active, you may be able to find school records.

Where Are the Archives?

If you do not find the records you want to see at the courthouse, they may have been transferred to central, state, or provincial archives. If so, microfilm copies are usually available for reference at the courthouse. Local libraries, historical and genealogical societies, and family history centers may also contain microfilmed copies and indexes.

What Else to Check on Location

While visiting your ancestor's previous county residence, check for microfilm of area newspapers during the period your ancestors lived there. Sometimes these are at the newspaper office, sometimes at the courthouse. In at least one county we found access to them only at the high school library.

While visiting your ancestor's previous county residence, check for microfilm of area newspapers during the period your ancestors lived there. Sometimes these are at the newspaper office, sometimes at the courthouse. In at least one county we found access to them only at the high school library.

Some family searchers gather only vital statistics such as birth, marriage, death, and spouse's name. Those are the "begats" again. Consequently, these researchers never try many other available sources, and they miss out on a lot of fun. They may not visit the local hometowns where much information and gossip can be heard.

In Texas, at the county abstract office, I met an elderly lady who had known my grandfather as a young man. She told me some tales I never heard before.

Almost every town has a small museum. These displays may vividly show you how your ancestors lived. You may even find a photograph or a story about your family.

TRUE STORY: In Illinois I found the only marriage record existing for an ancestor was a tiny three-sentence newspaper note: (*Fairfield Independent Press*, Apr 24, 1855) *Married on the 15th by John Morlan, Esq., Mr. Samuel Branch to Miss Lamy [sic] Ann Scott, all of this county.*

This item was difficult to read, as you can see in the copy on Figure 106. We could not be sure this was the right person until we found her unusual first name on a tombstone in a rural cemetery. After cleaning the stone, we were able to read: "Lamyh A. died 10 May 1863." Epitaph: "Died aged 26 yrs 7 mo 2 days, Wife of Samuel Branch."

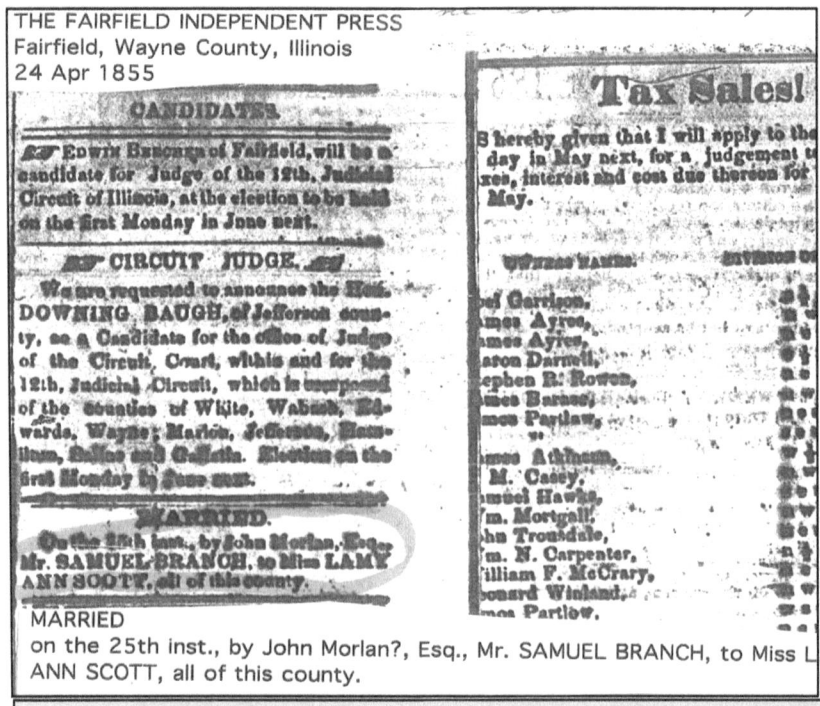

Figure 53: Newspaper announcement.

Sometimes, the only marriage record existing for an ancestor may be a tiny barely-readable newspaper note like this one. We found her grave marker in the rural cemetery near the family farm. Next to Lamyh Branch's grave we found a tiny tombstone. After cleaning we could read it too.

"Lamyh Ann, daughter of S & L.A. Branch, died 18 Aug 1863, aged 3 months 18 days."

Now we could put the missing pieces together. The husband went off to war in 1862, leaving a pregnant wife, Lamyh Ann, who died after giving birth. With the infant buried next to her, we could be sure this was Samuel's first wife. She died of childbirth complications while her husband was marching with the Illinois Infantry in the Civil War. The baby girl lived only three months.

Church Records

Church records can tell you about the births, baptisms, marriages, deaths, and burials of your ancestors, show transfers of membership, separation from the church, and may give hints in tracing a family's migration. Genealogists seem not to have realized their value; church records are among the most underused records. With so many denominations and changes in their structure over time genealogists cannot be blamed for hesitating to dive into that search.

My Dutch Reform ancestors were careful about recording every baptism from the 1600s to the 1800s in New Amsterdam, New Jersey, and Pennsylvania. Those records also name the parents and reveal the mother's maiden name. In most areas, church marriage records predate civil marriage records, except Puritans who believed marriage to be a civil ceremony. Church records differ greatly in content.

Two real difficulties with American church records are locating them and gaining access to them. Several years ago, when I learned my ancestor was a circuit-riding Methodist preacher, I wrote to the Central Illinois Conference, UM Church, Commission on Archives and History in Bloomington, Illinois, for confirmation. I received a reply with this information:

- "Geo W. Stribling was twice a probationer in this conference.
- 1835: First received, appointed to Shawneetown circuit, discontinued at next conference.
- 1839: Geo Stribling received again and assigned to Wabash Circuit in Vandalia district, the next year to Shawneetown Circuit, Mt Vernon District.
- In 1840 G.W. Stribling, returned 297 members.
- 1841 again discontinued at his own request."

In Summary

- ✓ Marriage bonds, licenses, and intentions are not evidence that a marriage occurred, only that a marriage was planned.
- ✓ In many marriage books, three different dates may be given:
- ✓ The date the couple got the license or bond,
- ✓ The date they married, and
- ✓ The date the marriage was filed.
- ✓ Some older books only give the date of the bond or license. Usually the wedding took place within a few days after that. Sometimes, for various reasons, the certificate was never recorded.
- ✓ The *Handy Book* offers addresses for you to write to the courthouses if you cannot go in person.
- ✓ Keep the letter brief and concise.
- ✓ Be specific about what you are requesting.
- ✓ Enclose a check and SASE.

Things to take with you to the courthouse:
- ✓ Family group sheets related to this county.
- ✓ Notes.
- ✓ Three ring binders of info you have collected.
- ✓ Your "Wish List" of the info you are seeking.
- ✓ Cash for copies.
- ✓ Pencils and notepad.
- ✓ A digital camera.

CHAPTER FIFTEEN

Books and Libraries

In colonial America, books were expensive and rare.

Generally, only the wealthy and the clergy owned more than one or two. Besides that, they had to order most books from London, and that quickly squelched literary curiosity. Books were so valuable in early America they were always inventoried right along with every stick of furniture and every head of livestock. Many things have changed in this two-hundred-plus years, but the value of learning remains, although now we take books and libraries for granted.

The following excerpt from the 1789 *Inventory of the Estate of the Rev. Cornelius Cosine*, deceased, of Conewago, York County, Pennsylvania, gives insight into the family status and education. Values show as they were at that time in the colonies; English pounds, shillings, pence. Rev. Cosine was a Dutch-speaking pastor, and obviously, he could also read and write English, at a time when many people could not even read one language. However, his wife could only sign with a mark.

Value in English pounds, shillings, pence.

21) one book by Wm Brocum 0.15.00

22) one book by ditto 0.15.00

23) one book by Sam' l Clark 0.15.00

24) one book Psalms 0.04.00
25) one book by Jacob Coleman 0.05.00
26) one book title Smitengale 0.15.00
27) one book Rutherford Letters 0.03.00
28) one book title Concordant 0.03.09
29) two books History [sic] 0.03.09
30) one book title Smitengale Sermons 0.02.09
31) one book Catechizing [Catechism] 0.07.06
32) one book Testament 0.03.09
33) one bookcase 0.01.00

Library History Buff Stuff

A statue of Athena, goddess of wisdom, stood at the entrance of the beautiful marble library of Ephesus, built in 117 A.D., reconstructed in the 1970s. Romans built the three-storied library at Ephesus, now in Turkey, more than three hundred years before Gutenberg invented the printing press. Twelve thousand book-rolls stacked inside on stone shelves. Scribes and leaders penned each scroll laboriously by hand.

About 300 B.C., Alexander the Great founded the Great Library of Alexandria in Egypt, a public library open only to those with the proper scholarly and literary qualifications.

Physically, books did not look like we see them today. Scribes and assistants shelved the scrolls, usually made of papyrus or leather, and filed them in pigeonholes. Titles written on wooden tags hung from their outer ends. When books were called for, assistants carried the scrolls in wooden buckets. The library in Alexandria, with all the knowledge of that age, burned in 48 BC in a fire which was probably caused by Julius Caesar.

Gutenberg's movable type innovation revolutionized bookmaking in the 1400s. Printed books stacked on open shelves replaced the handwritten manuscripts stored in pigeonholes.

The oldest library in America began in 1638 with a 400-book donation by a clergyman, John Harvard, to a new university in Massachusetts that honored him by adopting his name.

The British burned the infant Library of Congress during the War of 1812, leaving it in ashes. The library rebuilt three years later, with Thomas Jefferson's vast book collection filling the shelves.

Libraries with significant genealogical collections are an important place to conduct one's genealogical research, particularly once you have reached back four generations or more.

The first public library in the country opened in New Hampshire in 1833. Public libraries were hard to find until the twentieth century when Andrew Carnegie helped build more than 1,700 places of learning in the nation.

While libraries are not a new invention, they have changed over the years. No longer do pages carry scrolls in wooden buckets. The need for a repository of knowledge remains. During the post-Civil War years, newly formed women's clubs established many new public libraries. They contributed their collections of books, conducted lengthy fundraising campaigns for buildings, and lobbied within their communities for financial support.

More recently, libraries extend beyond the physical walls of a building by including material accessible by electronic means and by the assistance of librarians with a variety of digital tools.

Now we find both *circulating* libraries, where materials are loaned to patrons, institutions, or other libraries, and *collecting* libraries, where the materials are selected on the basis of their nature or subject matter. Many libraries are a mixture, containing a general collection for circulation and a more specialized reference collection not available for loan.

A Library Is a Library Is a Library—NOT!

The best sources are:
- Your state's historical society library.
- Local and county historical society libraries.

- University libraries.
- DAR and other lineage society libraries.
- County library, especially at the county seat town.
- LDS branch library.
- Family History Center (FHC) library.
- Private or special interest libraries.

Genealogy and historical libraries do not usually allow patrons to borrow books, but there are exceptions. Some do permit interlibrary loans.

Libraries with significant genealogical collections are an essential way to develop one's genealogical research, particularly once you have reached back four generations or more. Such library collections include compiled family histories and genealogies, local histories, and reference materials, which can be extremely helpful in your research. Also, most libraries have unique collections of unpublished documents, including such things as Bible records, surname files, etc.

The Family History Library in Salt Lake City

The most extensive collection of genealogical data is in Salt Lake City. Utah, in the library of The Church of Jesus Christ of Latter-Day Saints (LDS), sometimes called Mormons. As a result of their religious convictions, their genealogical collection is immense. Their resources are available to everyone; you do not need to be a member of their church. LDS maintains more than 2,500 Family History Centers across the country. These centers are usually not advertised, but you can ask any librarian at a public library, and they will be able to direct you.

If you are not near a public library, look in the white pages of the telephone directory to find The Church of Jesus Christ of Latter-Day Saints (LDS), then search for listings of local Family History Centers (FHC).

The LDS microfilming projects extend worldwide. Anyone can order microfilm for use in the FHC branches. Their computerized library catalog and other computer projects make access easy, even from your home computer.

Leaders of this group organized the Genealogical Society of Utah in 1894 to assist church members with their family history and genealogical research. The library and its Family History Centers have access to records from many governments, churches, and organizations. Only a small part of the collection is about the LDS church, its members, or their ancestors.

FamilySearch™ is a computerized system helping researchers identify their ancestors and organize family history information. You can access their website free at http://familysearch.org from your home computer.

The DAR Library in Washington

Outside of Salt Lake City, the best-known and most extensive library for genealogists is the Daughters of the American Revolution (DAR) Library in Washington, D.C. Most lineage society libraries, like DAR, are accessible by members only. If you have an interest in joining and can qualify with a direct ancestor who served the American Revolution cause, an existing member will be happy to sponsor your membership and assist you in your search for proof.

For more information, go to http://dar.org.

If you have a patriot (Revolutionary War Veteran or supporter) and want copies of information in his original documentation file without going to Washington, the fee is about $40 plus. If you would prefer to go to Washington to the DAR library to get the copies yourself, you have to jump through several hoops of security to get in. However, if you get in and find the record you want, instead of $40, you pay only for the copies. (Of course, the costs of travel do mount up!)

The Library of Congress in Washington

The Library of Congress (LC) has a vast genealogy department, but don't stop there. Go to: http://www.loc.gov/rr/ for a sample of what you can find in their online collections that include many governmental repositories. The LC online catalog opens the door to enter your family name in the search box. You probably won't find a book focusing on your household, but you might find a good book about your family surname. Try the same trick at FamilySearch.org. But, even if you should locate a book published with your family history included, do not assume everything in the book is correct.

The National Archives in Washington

The granddaddy of all libraries with the longest name: The Reference Library at National Archives and Records Administration (NARA), usually referred to just as the national archives. With a little help from a librarian, you can unlock some of the genealogical treasures hidden there. You may have ordered a copy of your ancestor's military record but missed the copies of Bible records and handwritten notes on the backsides of papers. Study the catalog on their website before you go. We are all genealogical detectives on a quest to unearth our ancestors and the documents that tell us about them. http://www.archives.gov

The Allen County Library in Indiana

The Allen County Public Library at Ft. Wayne, Indiana, has one of the largest collections of genealogy materials in the nation with many thousands of genealogy books of all descriptions. Librarians experienced in genealogical research are always on duty to answer your questions. Type "Allen County Public Library genealogy" in your browser to search, or go directly to the URL:
http://www.acpl.lib.in.us/genealogy/index.html

New England Genealogical Library

If you have New England ancestry, check with the New England Historic Genealogical Society (NEHGS) http://www.newenglandancestors.org. Founded in 1845, NEHGS is the oldest and most respected nonprofit genealogical organization in the country. At one time, this was the only genealogical library that would lend books to members. Now many older reference books are online and available to all.

Do your homework before you go

I do not recommend that novices make a trip to any of these large centers until you have done a lot of homework and preparation.

TRUE STORY: We made a trip to the Netherlands where I could research my Low Dutch ancestry. My ancestor had immigrated in the 1600s to New Amsterdam, now New York City. We had a wonderful time touring historic Holland and The Netherlands, but I was never able to locate or spend any time at one of their genealogical libraries; also, the language barrier prevented me from reading the Dutch documents. We met a banker who was interested in genealogy, and he offered to take my family history sheet to the library in Amsterdam to gather information for me.

A month or two after we returned home, I received the family history sheet in the mail, unchanged from when I had given it to the man. A note attached said, *"The librarian said for you to go to Salt Lake City in the USA. They have all the records there."*

Libraries Everywhere, USA

All states have a primary historical library or repository. Sometimes you may find not just a library but also a state genealogical society research library, a state archives with a library, or a state historical society research center. These collections may include old newspaper archives, manuscripts, both published and unpublished, microfilm collections, military records, and a large number of family history volumes. Go there and make friends with the librarians and volunteers who know where the skeletons and useful data hides.

Volunteers can explain that particular library's cataloging system—many have their own system in addition to the Dewey Decimal System. You usually find a standard card catalog with entries by subject, title, and author, as well as lists of newspapers, schools, photographs, and biographies of local personalities. Most of this information is now on the computer because the card catalog might fill one room by itself in large libraries.

Many have published their catalogs online or in hard copies, such as the Newberry Library in Chicago, the New York Public Library, and others. The Library of Congress offers an index of genealogies in their collection. Another essential source is *Genealogical and Local History Books in Print,* with thousands of books listed and updated regularly. These indexes should be available at your local historical or genealogical society library.

Finding Your Way with Books

Hundreds of genealogy and history periodicals are helpful to researchers. Some libraries now have PERSI— the Periodical Source Index—available on Heritage Quest or on CD-ROM.

CD-ROM, pronounced *see-dee-rom,* is short for Compact Disc-Read-Only Memory, a type of optical disk capable of storing large amounts of data. Ask your librarian what they have available. As you may be noticing, it helps to make the reference librarian your new best friend.

TRUE STORY: In the past, I have found treasures in each type of library. Some of the most valuable information turned up in a college library in Athens, Ohio. I learned my sixth-great-grandfather donated land for the University, because I stumbled onto that record while looking for something else.

Be sure to detail in your research log the date of your trip, the name and address of the library visited, and in which book or file you found specific information so that you can find it again. Whenever possible, I make a copy of the book page(s), the title page, and copyright information, just in case.

Where's the Book with My Family's History?

Often a new genealogist will expect to end their search quickly and find their family tree and history already done. That is probably possible, but I don't know of any such instances. You can find hundreds of published and unpublished family histories at public libraries, in historical and genealogical societies and on the Internet.

When traveling in the area where your ancestors lived, visit as many libraries as possible. I found some great family information in a small-town library in Kansas.

In Summary

Many types of libraries can help in your search:
- ✓ Public libraries,
- ✓ Private libraries,
- ✓ Genealogical libraries,
- ✓ Historical Society libraries,
- ✓ Lending libraries,
- ✓ University and college libraries,
- ✓ Church-based libraries,
- ✓ Lineage society libraries such as the DAR library,
- ✓ The voluminous LDS library in Salt Lake City,
- ✓ The National Archives.
- ✓ Small town libraries.
- ✓ Review all published genealogies carefully, as many are inaccurate.

CHAPTER SIXTEEN

Maps and Migration Patterns

Maps are your friends.

Geography is important! When your ancestors suddenly disappear from the records of the county where they had been living, they may have hit the road on the westward migration.

TRUE STORY: In 1767, my Low Dutch ancestors, who had settled New Amsterdam in the 1600s, suddenly disappeared from New York and New Jersey. One short paragraph in a New Jersey county history book explained it. "...more than a hundred Dutch Reformed Church families moved west to the Conewago Valley near Gettysburg, York County, Pennsylvania, in the mid-to-late 1700s. This one-hundred-fifty-mile journey mostly on foot took them three weeks."

Sure enough, I found my people and their Dutch Reformed community in York County, Pennsylvania.

And then they disappeared again.

Even before 1783, when the Revolutionary War officially ended, the Low Dutch group began their move to the wild Kentucky frontier – they called it Cain-tuck-ee.

They had two choices of paths to Kentucky—the Wilderness Trail or the River Road—either way a long, hard journey full of danger. These stalwart pioneers did not let that stop them.

The Ohio River Route followed the river from Pittsburgh (then Fort Pitt) on to the Falls of the Ohio, just above Louisville.

In the book, "*Banta Pioneers ...*" by Elsa M. Banta (1983) and "*A Supplement to Banta Pioneers ...*" (1985), page 185 (used by permission), the author gives details from family journals about the trip down Wilderness Road through the newly opened Cumberland Gap:

"Men were on foot with their long rifles on their shoulders, driving stock and leading packhorses. The women, some walking with pails on their heads, others riding with children in their laps, and some children swinging in baskets on horses. The women shouldered equal if different responsibilities with their men.

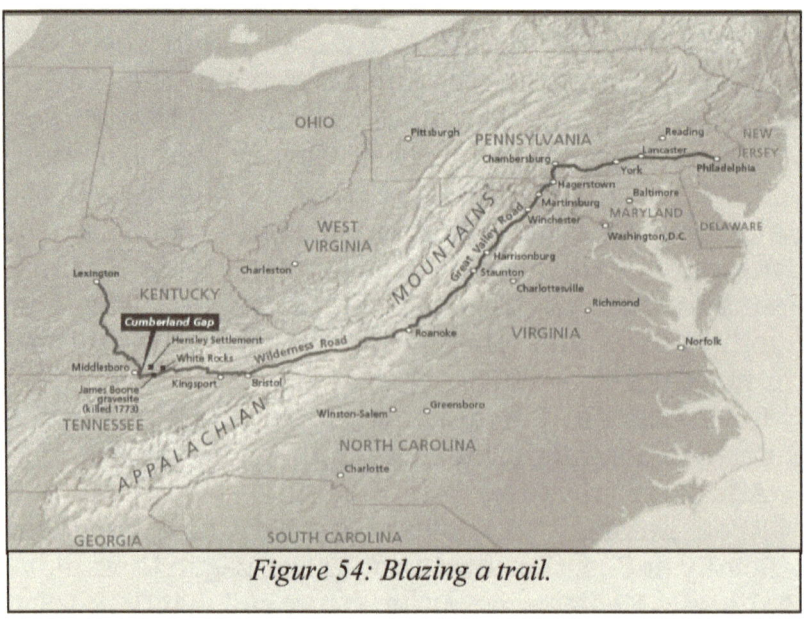

Figure 54: Blazing a trail.

"The group existed on small allowances of stale bread and meat. They encountered bears, wolves and wild cats in the narrow bridle path overgrown with

brush and briars. Yet they continued their perilous journey with no thought of abandoning it."

How fascinating to read such a description and imagine the scene from those details. Maps provide clues to where ancestors lived, difficulties of travel, how settlements evolved, and where to look for written records.

The long, long trail

Beginning at Long Island on the Holston River, Daniel Boone and his men in 1775 blazed a trail through 200 miles of Virginia wilderness to the Cumberland Gap. This trail became the main road for pioneers heading west.

The United States Geological Survey (USGS) has been producing maps since being founded in 1879. These include topographic maps, aerial photographs, satellite imagery, maps of mines, geology, land use, energy, earthquakes, floods, ecoregions, and much more. Locating the name of a place where an ancestor lived can be like trying to hit a moving target. That is when old maps become particularly useful. Many towns, counties, cities, and even countries have gone through name changes over the years, and many communities disappeared.

Never, ever give up

Don't give up! Though their names have changed, you might still find some of these places on an old map. For instance, old Indian Territory maps of Oklahoma showing the location of early forts and frontier settlements are being re-published now. See <http://okmaps.library.okstate.edu>

With just a click of your mouse, you can zoom in and see how the state and nation looked to mapmakers two hundred years ago.

You might find the location of some no-longer-existing towns in other sources such as lists of abandoned post offices, local histories, government records, microfilm records, old newspapers, old city directories, or old county atlases kept in the library archives of a town, city, or county in the region.

Constantly changing place names are not the only challenge; the boundaries of many political jurisdictions where early Americans lived may have moved once or twice. Some American families lived in the same locale for hundreds of years, yet their homes swapped back and forth between different political jurisdictions—towns, provinces, even states, or countries.

A book that can be extremely helpful here is *Map Guide to the U.S. Federal Censuses 1790–1920* by William Thorndale and William Dollarhide.

TRUE STORY: When my Dutch ancestors first migrated to the Kentucky frontier in 1781, it was still a county in Virginia. By 1790, Kentucky County, Virginia, had nine subdivisions. Statehood came in 1792. In the 1800 census, my relatives still lived on the same piece of land, although their land descriptions had changed several times. Less than a dozen years after moving to the unorganized frontier, they were living in a new state divided into about 35 counties.

Land has ancestors, too!

I wish we could go to a website that would show the rotating county lines for various counties in the different census years, overlaid with past and present maps so you can see how county boundaries changed.

If you find unfamiliar place names during your search, the U.S. Geological Survey can help. (See contact info below)

The *Geographic Names Information System (GNIS)* is the nation's official database of place names. The GNIS, maintained by the U.S. Geological Survey (USGS), can often provide information on name changes. This database contains two million entries, including the names of places that no longer exist, as well as variant names for current locations.

This automated system also contains the names of every type of feature except roads and highways. It is especially useful for genealogical research because it includes entries for communities, as well as for churches and cemeteries, even those that no longer exist.

To use this free service, email:
gnis_manager@usgs.gov
Telephone 703-648-4544

You can also visit the GNIS Web site:
www.geonames.usgs.gov

Once you've used maps to identify the most likely place names for your ancestors' homes, try a local library or historical society to find atlases, gazetteers, local directories, and other sources that pertain to locales of interest.

In Summary

- ✓ Maps and geography are essential to genealogy.
- ✓ Early migration trails can be located and studied.
- ✓ People moved from east to west and to, some extent, north to south.
- ✓ Early pioneers often were limited to packhorses.
- ✓ As trails widened, wagons were put to use, hauled by teams of horses or oxen.
- ✓ Go to: www.cyndislist.com/migration.htm for help locating maps.

CHAPTER SEVENTEEN

Was Great-Grandpa a Soldier?

Military Records

Most of the records of the American Army and Navy were destroyed in 1800 and again in 1814. The War Department began a project in 1894 to rebuild that information, creating individual packets from a variety of sources for each soldier. These are called Compiled Military Service Records, and they are available; however, these records are of limited genealogical value except to prove military service. For more about access to military records, go to this website: https://www.archives.gov/veterans

War creates lots of paper that can be helpful to genealogists. Check out any major conflicts during which your ancestor lived and apply for copies of pension records. These often contain valuable family history.

Estimate your ancestor's age, and if he was between ages sixteen and sixty in the 1776-1783 period, look for a Revolutionary War service record. Many soldiers served even younger than age sixteen. A promise of bounty land, in addition to or instead of pay, induced older men to enlist as well.

Bounty Land from Federal and States

Bounty land is "public land" awarded by the federal government under certain conditions to veterans for their service in the military in earlier years. Bounty land warrants became a substitute for wages because Congress did not have funds to pay its soldiers. The application files often contain information similar to the genealogically-rich pension files. In addition to federal service bounty grants, nine states also paid their state militia soldiers with bounty land: Connecticut, Georgia, Maryland, Massachusetts, New York, North Carolina, Pennsylvania, South Carolina, and Virginia.

A citizen militia was economical. The soldiers brought their equipment, and they got paid only when called to duty. Theoretically, all male citizens from their late teens to their fifties were liable for service in the militia, although wealthy men could hire substitutes to serve in their place.

The militia turned out about two or three times a year for drilling and training, although some reports sound as if they practiced drinking whiskey and gambling more often than military tactics.

Almost all the citizenry participated, on one side or the other, in the Revolutionary conflict. A person who provided or transported supplies, oversaw roads, served on a safety committee, or provided additional support for the revolution was considered a patriot. Keep in mind, your ancestors—at least some of them—for various reasons may have leaned toward supporting the King (Loyalists) rather than the Rebels (Continentals). Much like the later U.S. Civil War, these battles divided families, friends, and neighbors—sometimes forever. Wealthy citizens were more likely pro-British.

Let's focus on the Revolutionary War (1775-1783), the War of 1812, and the Civil War (1861-1865), although these are not the only military record collections.

The DAR (Daughters of the American Revolution) webpage has excellent information on Revolutionary War Veterans. Type www.dar.org in your browser and click on Patriot Index Lookup to see if someone has already done the work of proving your ancestor's service. Enter the required information about yourself and as much as you know about your ancestor. There is no charge for this service.

The DAR Patriot Index contains names of Revolutionary patriots, both men and women, whose service between 1775 and

1783 is proven by the National Society of the Daughters of the American Revolution. Additional data available may include dates and places of birth and death, name(s) of wife (wives) or husband(s), rank, type of service, and the state where the patriot lived or served. If they find your person's pension papers, they will tell you how to purchase a copy. These records, like most others, are not infallible. If they do not find the name you are seeking, do not be discouraged. That only means no one has yet proved your ancestor's service.

At the close of the Revolutionary War, the United States government began administering a limited pension system to soldiers wounded during active military service or veterans and their widows pleading dire poverty. By the 1830s military pensions became available to all surviving veterans or their widows. Don't get your hopes up too high. You may find a forty-page pension file, or it might turn up just a bare-bones military record.

Birth years of Men and Wars when They May Have Served*

Born Between	War	Date of War
1560-1760	Colonial Wars	1607-1774
1720-1763	American Revolution	1775-1783
1740-1791	Indian Wars	1790-1800
1762-1894	War of 1812	1812-1815
1762-1840	Indian Wars	1815-1858
1796-1828	Mexican War	1846-1848
1806-1849	Civil War	1861-1865
1848-1884	Spanish-American War	1898-1902
1865-1900	World War I	1914-1918
1891-1927	World War II	1941-1945
1900-1936	Korean War	1950-1953
1915-1953	Viet Nam War	1965-1973

*Chart from "Finding Military Records" by Billie Stone Fogarty ©2009, Used by permission.

Treasures in the National Archives

Genealogists hope for all three types of records:

1. Military service records,
2. Pension claim files, and
3. Bounty-land warrant applications.

Pension application files are quite valuable to genealogists. The government granted pensions only to those who could provide proof of service and meet other eligibility requirements. In those records, you may uncover affidavits made by close friends or relatives, and these affidavits often contain extensive family history.

A widow's application usually contains more genealogical information than a veteran's file. In addition, there may be depositions proving his service, his birthplace, his age, and his place of residence. The widow had to furnish the date and place of her marriage to the veteran, her maiden name, age and home address, the veteran's date and place of death, and the names and ages of any minor children. Often a relative signed as a witness, giving you another clue to follow in your investigation.

Footnote and Ancestry

Footnote.com, as discussed earlier, is an excellent resource to find pension records as well as old deeds, court records, and military papers. With the sharp increase in the cost of acquiring military documents from the National Archives, The Internet site "Footnote" is a welcome relief to historians. Some libraries may offer the use of their Footnote subscription to holders of their library card. If you are not close enough to use a library, the amount of time and effort you save in searching might be well worth the cost of a subscription. Some services will allow you to join free for a limited time; some will not. Footnote will enable you to see a thumbnail image of records containing your ancestor's name, but you must join and pay to download the full record—unless you are at a participating library.

You can always read the microfilm of Revolutionary War pension files and bounty land warrant applications at your local FHC or the state historical library where you can print them out for the cost of copies.

The War Between the States

Brother fighting against brother, families ripped asunder, children left fatherless. Whether your family dressed in blue or gray, the stories are much the same. It was all about destruction.

However, if your Union soldier lived long enough, chances are good he applied for a federal pension. The earliest pensions went to families of those disabled or killed. Pensions for Confederate soldiers are not plentiful.

The name of the war depended on your political leanings. The War Between the States was also known as the Civil War, War of The Rebellion, War of Northern Aggression.

Union States: California, Connecticut, Illinois, Indiana, Iowa, Kansas, Maine, Massachusetts, Michigan, Minnesota, New Hampshire, New Jersey, New York, Ohio, Oregon, Pennsylvania, Rhode Island, Vermont, and Wisconsin.

Confederate States: Alabama, Arkansas, North and South Carolina, Florida, Georgia, Louisiana, Mississippi, Tennessee, and Texas.

Mixed States: Four border states did not secede, and many residents served on different sides: Delaware, Kentucky, Maryland, and Missouri. The counties in West Virginia separated from the state of Virginia in 1861 and was admitted to the Union in 1863. However, the number of sympathizers remained somewhat equal on both sides of the conflict.

Confederate Pensions

The National Archives and Records Administration (NARA) web site, www.archives.gov, holds original pension records for Union veterans but not Confederate pensions, because money for the south's soldiers came from their home states, not through the federal government. The Confederate veteran was eligible to apply for a pension to the state in which he then lived, even if he served in a unit from a different one. Even then, not all soldiers or their widows requested a pension.

Generally, an applicant was eligible for a pension only if he was indigent or disabled. Destitute widows may have applied for a pension based on their husbands' service. Whether the pension was granted or denied, the file can contain useful information including birth, death, and marriage dates as well as affidavits from family and friends.

For additional information regarding Confederate pension files, contact the state archives for the state where the veteran lived at the time he would have become eligible for a pension.

Confederate soldiers were supported entirely at the state level with no funds from the federal government against which they had fought. States that paid Confederate pensions were Alabama, Arkansas, Florida, Georgia, Louisiana, Mississippi, and Texas.

The *Confederate Veteran Magazine,* 1893-1932, published obituaries and photographs of veterans or family members. You can find a searchable index here:

http://www.lva.virginia.gov/public/guides/opac/aboutvetmagazine.htm

TRUE STORY: Searching the Montgomery County, Virginia, website, I discovered an exciting insight to the re-construction period after the war:

The Claim of George Surface of Montgomery Co in the State of Virginia.

April 10, 1865
1 horse ------------ $125.00   (item 1)
1 horse ------------ $100.00   (item 2)
1 mare ------------ $85.00   (item 3)
1 horse ------------ $95.00   (item 4)

TOTAL ------------- $405.00

Mr. Surface does not remember how he voted on the Ordinance of Secession. "Son says he voted for secession." The poll list shows he did vote for secession. He had two sons in the rebel Army. Had $300 in confederate bonds. Loyalty is not proved.

The papers were stamped: **Claim rejected**

"TO: Commissioner of Claims
Affidavit: I took the Amnesty oath after the war. I had nothing to be pardoned for. I had a horse taken by the rebels and received no pay for it. I had a [second] horse taken when sixteen Rebel soldiers came to my house and threatened to arrest me on account of my Union sentiments. I fed rebel deserters and harbored them. I had two sons in the rebel Army. I gave them no Army or Military equipment. They were both married men. I had 300 dollars in Confederate Bonds. I did nothing else to support. I was a Union man all the time. I don't know how I voted upon the ordinance of Secession. There was a threat made that if we did not vote for it, we would have to leave the State in 30 days. My son told me I voted for it. After it passed, I still adhered to the Union. From the beginning to the end of the war, I desired the success of the Union in putting down the rebellion. I was willing to do all I could to accomplish that end. And further the deponent sayeth not.
(signed) George Surface
Sworn and subscribed to this 29th of April 1873."

Affidavits by neighbors attesting to the truth of these statements follow, but the Union still denied his claim for relief.

An inventory of the United Confederate Veterans Association is online at:
    wwwlib,lsuedu/special/findaid/u1357.html

Civil War Soldiers and Sailors System

An online database of servicemen from this war called the Civil War Soldiers and Sailors System is here:

www.civilwar.nps.gov/cwss/. Click on the appropriate branch of service to search for your person by name.

This database lists Union and Confederate servicemen along with some information about their service. You will find other information about cemeteries, battles, unit histories, prisoners, medals of honor, and more.

The original service records of Union and Confederate Civil War Soldiers and the pension records of Union veterans remain at the National Archives Building in Washington, DC, where they are available for research.

The service records exist in both their initially created form and on microfilm; however, the pensions are only on microfilm. When searching the pension index, try variations in spelling the name. Most pensions are listed as "Invalid." That does not mean they refused the annuity. The word is pronounced *in*valid, such as a person with a medical disorder. Veterans must be disabled and unable to work to qualify for a subsidy.

Once you find your veteran ancestor on the index, you can order the record by going in person to the National Archives or by filling out Form NATF-85, downloadable online at this website: http://www.archives.gov/contact/inquire-form.html

Allow up to three months to receive your order. You can save a step by putting credit card information on the form. The Archives will not charge your card until they have the file in hand.

The military service records and pension files are separate series of records. They must be requested separately. For example, if you need both the service record and the pension file for one particular veteran who fought for the Union, you need to submit two separate orders. Sometimes the pension file includes personal information and details of experiences in service, which adds significantly to your knowledge of their lives.

TRUE STORY: Pension files I received for two Union soldiers (not related) contained physical descriptions. One had red hair, ruddy complexion, and stood five feet nine inches tall. The other had black hair, gray eyes, light complexion, and measured five feet eleven inches tall. The pension file described battles they were in and injuries they received. A pension file for a third veteran revealed no personal description and only sparse details of his service.

How Did They Qualify for Pension?

In 1861, shortly after the Civil War began, Congress needed to attract recruits to the military. Legislators enacted legislation providing pensions for Union soldiers who suffered war-related disabilities, as well as widows and orphans of soldiers killed in action.

Congress amended the law in 1862 to provide a maximum pension of $8 per month for total disability with proportionately reduced awards for partial disability.

Widows and orphans also qualified, and amendments to the law increased the allowance to widows by $2 per dependent child. Where a veteran left no widow or children, the law provided benefits to dependent mothers or sisters. Eventually, if the veteran had no dependent mother or sister, dependent fathers and brothers were included.

The law was amended repeatedly in the 1860s, 1870s, and 1880s. Amendments increased pension amounts over the years and extended the program to veterans with disabilities that developed after the war, if the cause stemmed from wartime injuries.

In 1890 Congress enacted a new law that paid pensions to any Union veteran of the Civil War who served for at least ninety days, was honorably discharged, and suffered from a disability, even if not war-related.

In 1904 the Spanish-American War Rough Rider veteran, President Theodore "Teddy" Roosevelt, ruled that old age itself was a disability, basically transforming the system into a government pension system for all Civil War veterans.

The Teddy Roosevelt Years, 1901-1909

As an aside and an example of the period, President Theodore "Teddy" Roosevelt worked to ensure the government improved the lives of American citizens.

Vice President Roosevelt moved into the office at age 43 on the 1901 assassination of William McKinley. Teddy still holds the record as the nation's youngest president.

Oklahoma, in 1907 became the only new state to enter the union during the TR years. His "Square Deal" domestic program reflected the progressive call to reform the American workplace, initiating welfare legislation and government regulation of industry. He was also the nation's first environmentalist president, setting aside nearly 200 million acres for national forests, reserves, and wildlife refuges. Teddy Bears got their name from TR's enjoyment of hunting expeditions.

Figure 55: Theodore Roosevelt

The nation had never known a family in the White House, quite like Teddy Roosevelts crew. The public loved to follow the adventures of the Roosevelt clan; the President understood that his family was a political asset and made it available, to some degree, to the media.

After the sudden death of his first wife, Roosevelt married Edith Kermit Carow. He already had a daughter, Alice, from his first marriage. He and Edith had five more children—Theodore, Kermit, Edith, Archibald, and Quentin. For TR, his family was like having his own private circus. His children were everywhere, having the complete run of the place. They took their favorite pony, Algonquin, into the White House elevator, frightened visiting officials with a four-foot king snake and dropped water balloons on the heads of White House guards.

Old Soldiers' Homes

The states established and operated their soldiers' homes with state monies following the Civil War. The Veterans

Administration (VA), a federal agency, did not replace the system, although in some cases, the agency acquired the buildings now vacant. The Old Soldiers' Home in Washington (renamed the Armed Forces Retirement Home) remains in continuous use since its establishment in 1851 as the first national old soldiers' home, funded through monthly contributions from pay of members of the U.S. Armed Services.

The pension applications and records from the Old Soldiers' Homes are quite detailed. Here's an example:

TRUE STORY: The seven sons of Abraham V. Dudrey enlisted in the Union army from Wayne County, Illinois, in 1861, including William Dudrey, only sixteen years old at enlistment. From the Illinois State archives at Springfield, he is listed as five feet seven inches tall with dark hair and dark complexion, serving in Company M, Fifth Illinois Cavalry.

By the age of 36 when Pvt. Dudrey entered the facility, he was a widower and a total invalid. His wife died of TB the year before. Unable to work to support his family, he gave his three young children up for adoption. He was receiving a pension of $6 a month when he died at age 45. He is buried in the National Cemetery at Leavenworth.

Figure 56: Pvt. Wm Dudrey 1862

This transcribed report came from records of the "Old Soldiers' Home" at Leavenworth, Kansas.

1882, General Affidavit on Pension Claim # 362687:

"I am the identical William Dudrey, named in the above-cited case. I am not able to furnish the testimony of Commissioned officers or my 1st Sgt as to proof of origin in line of duty of the incurrence of bloody piles, my disability, for the reason I have not been able to find the whereabouts of any having personal knowledge of same, wherefore I ask that the testimony of comrade Levi Branch and that of RBR Feather corroborating this be accepted in lieu of such.

I had no treatment in the service for alleged disability, except attending sick call a few times and some medicine. [I] don't remember the surgeon's name. If I did, he would not remember me, as I had no acquaintance with him ... I contracted the illness near Camp LaFayette in ... Tennessee in May 1865 and have suffered continuously ever since ... greatly disabled ... at least half incapacitated ... last five years totally disabled, often bleeding so that I could not do anything and ... had to enter the Old Soldiers Home." [National Military Home, Leavenworth, KS]

Figure 57: Wm Dudrey, Ft Leavenworth Cemetery.\, KS.

[signed]*William Dudrey*

Veteran's Administration, Leavenworth, KS

Many abandoned buildings at the Old Soldiers' Home near Leavenworth, Kansas, are now the property of the Veteran's Administration. Once a beautiful, peaceful place where old soldiers from the Civil War era lived out their lives in the company of their comrades-at-arms, the facility is now in shambles.

Many of the original such institutions across the United States, like the now-deserted Leavenworth facility, appeared in high Victorian style. It was not unusual for old soldiers to live out their old age, pass on in the infirmary, and be laid to rest with honors in the adjoining cemetery, as was Civil War Veteran William Dudrey, who died here in 1890.

In 1866 Union veterans of the Civil War organized into the Grand Army of the Republic and became a social and political force that controlled the destiny of the nation for more than six decades. The organization wielded considerable political clout nationwide. Between 1868 and 1908, no Republican was nominated to the presidency without a GAR endorsement.

Based partly on traditions of Freemasonry and partly on military culture, the organization divided into "departments" at the state level and "posts" at the community level, with posts in every state in the nation and several overseas. Members wore military-style uniforms.

The Grand Army of the Republic was the first genuinely national Veterans organization in the country. The SUVCW (Sons of Union Veterans of the Civil War) and the DUVCW (Daughters of Union Veterans of the Civil War) are allied orders.

The war brought men together from different communities and different states by the necessities of battle. They forged new friendships and lasting trust. With advances in care and movement of the wounded, many who would have died in earlier wars returned home. A community, now also faced with the needs of widows and orphans, would have to care for them.

GAR (Grand Army of the Republic)

One of the little-known military organizations that may have information about your ancestor is the Grand Army of the Republic (GAR), organized by Union veterans after the Civil War. If you find a GAR marker on your ancestor's grave, you know there is a military record somewhere.

Probably the most profound emotion these soldiers shared was emptiness. Men who had lived together, fought together, foraged together and survived, developed a unique unbreakable bond. Friendships forged in battle survived the separation, and the warriors missed the warmth of trusting companionship that asked only total and absolute commitment.

Veterans needed jobs, including a whole new unique group of veterans—the black soldier and his newly freed family. State and federal leaders from President Lincoln down promised to care for "those who have borne the burden, his widows and orphans," but they had little knowledge of how to accomplish the task.

In the early years, each post filed quarterly reports of new members, suspensions, drops, transfers, and deaths of their members. As membership dropped, reports first became semiannual and finally annual.

Best known for their encampments held across the country, their final gathering of the Grand Army of the Republic convened in Indianapolis in 1949. The last member, Albert Woolson, died in 1956 at the age of 109 years.

Andy Waskie, historian of the GAR museum in Philadelphia, said recently that most of the GAR records remained local, with National Encampment Reports the only ones retained at the museum. "Those records cite very few names of local post members, only national officers," Waskie said. The museum does hold a few post records from Pennsylvania and New York.

Their address is 4278 Griscom St, Philadelphia 19124-3954. Phone: (215)289-6484 Email: garmuslib@verizon.net or go to their Facebook page: GAR Museum and Library in Philadelphia.

Waskie suggested reading the May 30th (Decoration Day) articles from year to year in the newspaper where your ancestor lived. Most newspapers wrote about activities of the local GAR post observing the holiday. Often member names are listed for those marching in the parades. The GAR museum would like to have copies of any records you find.

Membership in GAR, the Union veterans' organization, was restricted to individuals who had served in the Army, Navy, Marine Corps, or Revenue Cutter Service during the Civil War, thereby limiting the life span of the GAR. Started with just fourteen members, the organization grew to 400,000 Union veterans dedicated to preserving the memory of their fallen comrades.

Is Great-Grandpa on the GAR List?

Lists of Colorado and Nebraska GAR members are online at http://denverlibrary.org/. You must search that site, because the address changes. The collection supposedly consists of roll books, financial ledgers, adjutant's reports, meeting minutes, descriptive texts, and death records from the various posts in the department of Colorado and Wyoming.

About 1880, GAR annual reports at the state level began listing members who died during the previous year. These death rolls might show the veteran's name, wartime unit, age at death, date of death, and the local post he had joined.

Some GAR records are online at the Kansas Historical Society web site: www.KSHS.org, or you could just search online for GAR Necrologies.

For more information on the published GAR rolls, visit www.ngpublications.com/index.htm. These sources will not replace 1890 census information, but they may help you locate an obituary, death certificate, probate record, or other information you need.

In Summary:

- ✓ Most records of the U.S. Army and Navy were destroyed in 1800 and 1814.
- ✓ There are many little-known wars in which your ancestors may have participated.
- ✓ Civil War Pension records are a treasure trove to genealogists.
- ✓ Old Soldiers' Home records and GAR records may have info on your Union veteran ancestor.
- ✓ The final member of the G.A.R. to pass, Albert Woolson, died in 1956.

Figure 58: The long-abandoned Old Soldiers home, Dorm, & chapel at Leavenworth, KS, in 2008.

The neighing troop, the flashing blade,
The bugle's stirring blast,
The charge, the dreadful cannonade,
The din and shout are past.

Figure 59: GAR symbols.

CHAPTER EIGHTEEN

What about DNA

DNA can provide clues about your ethnic origin.

Not long ago, few people would have speculated that every cell nucleus in the human body contains the genetic master code for the entire human being as if every room in the multi-chambered Pentagon held the architectural plans for the complete structure.

Wouldn't it be wonderful if you knew what genetic medical conditions you may have inherited from your ancestors? Then you could take measures to stave off, or even prevent, the onset of disease?

With the availability of millions of genetic markers in DNA, biomedical researchers now believe that such exciting medical advances are not that far away.

DNA or deoxyribonucleic acid is the hereditary material in humans and almost all other organisms. The cell nucleus holds the most DNA. Nearly every cell in a person's body contains the same DNA. Most experts say every other human is close to being your identical twin, with people worldwide sharing almost one hundred percent of the natural human DNA sequence.

Genealogical DNA tests generally involve comparing the results of living individuals because you cannot conveniently obtain samples from deceased ancestors.

While it can't provide you with your entire family tree or tell you who your ancestors are, DNA testing can:
- Determine if two people are related.
- Determine if two people descend from a common ancestor.
- Find out if you are related to others with the same surname.
- Prove or disprove some family tree legends.
- Provide clues about your ethnic origin.

DNA tests have been around for many years. Still, only recently has the cost of genetic testing finally came down into the realm of possibility for the average individual interested in tracing his roots. The results always seem to require a minimum of a biology degree.

The key to the genealogical use of DNA is principally the Y chromosome, which only passes down the male line from father to son. If you are female, you need to convince a brother, father, paternal uncle, or another lineal descendant with the family surname you want to trace to do the DNA testing for you.

The DNA test traces only that one surname passed down from father to son along with the Y chromosome. DNA testing relies on unbroken male lineages. It can be foiled at any time by unknown breaks in the bloodline, called non-paternal events (NPE). Sources of "breaks" might include:
- Hanky-panky with the neighbor,
- A pregnant bride marrying the wrong man, or
- Unrecorded adoptions.

Home DNA test kits can be ordered through the mail or over the Internet at a cost averaging $100-$400 per test, with the price dropping as testing becomes more prevalent. Ancestry.com offers Y-DNA tests for as low as $79. The test is not complicated, usually consisting of a cheek swab to quickly collect a sample of cells from the inside of your mouth. Some laboratories use mouthwash or chewing gum instead of cheek swabs. Some laboratories offer to store DNA samples for ease of future testing. Others will destroy the DNA sample upon request by the customer, guaranteeing that the gene will not be available for further analysis.

You send back the sample through the mail, and within a month or two, you receive the results. The segments of DNA on the Y chromosome, found only in males, are referred to as genetic markers. These markers can then be compared to results from other individuals to help you determine your ancestry.

Here's Some Technical Stuff You Can Skip

You may need to learn the language, including acronyms, to follow along. Y-DNA tests generally examine 10-67 STR markers on the Y chromosome, but more than a hundred are available. A single nucleotide polymorphism, or SNP, pronounced "snip," is a small genetic change or variation that can occur within a person's DNA sequence. SNP results indicate the haplogroup. A chromosome contains sequences of repeating nucleotides known as short tandem repeats (STRs). The number of repetitions varies from one person to another. STR test results provide the haplotype.

A panel of twenty-two SNPs provides backbone haplogroup placement. Results identify the ethnic and geographic origin of the maternal line.

So, roughly defined, a **haplotype** is a set of numbers or letters obtained from the DNA test of an individual. A **haplogroup** is a group of similar patterned and related descendant haplotypes that share a common ancestor.

Although many SNPs do not produce physical changes in people, scientists believe that other SNPs may predispose people to disease and influence their response to drug regimens. By studying stretches of DNA that have been found to harbor the SNP related to a disease trait, researchers may begin to reveal relevant genes associated with a disease.

What will you learn from the results?

By using average marker mutation rates, Family Tree DNA database claims it is possible to compare two profiles and back-calculate how long ago their most recent common ancestor lived. They admit the method came from anthropological science, and although of some use, it has a margin of error that reduces its usefulness in individual family history studies.

More recently, the Y chromosome in the nuclear DNA establishes family ties. Tiny chemical markers on the Y chromosome create a distinctive pattern, known as a haplotype, that distinguishes one male lineage from another. Shared markers can indicate relatedness between two men, though not the exact degree of the relationship.

How Many Markers do you need?

We paid for an upgrade to 25 markers and later moved up to 37. You pay for the test according to the number of these you want. The higher the number tested, the more accurate your results. At first, we picked only twelve markers. Soon we received hundreds of notices of perfect 12 for 12 matches; however, matching DNA doesn't mean much unless the surname is the same. None of those matches came with our same name.

TRUE STORY: I talked my brother into doing the DNA test for our paternal family line. At that time, there were only two others in the group.

My brother's twelve-marker DNA test did not match with the other family contributor DNA on file at that lab. We are even from a different haplogroup (location of origin). I was beginning to wonder, *Are we really who we think we are?*

Then an email arrived from a man named Andrew Grisham. He was planning to do the test and submit it to our family group. I patiently explained that it would not work because you must share the same surname.

He said, "Didn't you know Branch and Grisham are the same families? A knight named Sir Peter de Branche served under William the Conqueror in 1066. After winning the battle, the Conqueror awarded Sir Peter de Branche the village of Gresham for his participation. Sir Peter had two sons, Nicholas and Roger. Nicholas retained the surname of de Branche (later Branch), and Roger assumed the name de Gresham."

That sounded familiar. (See the previous reference to this same story in Chapter 10.) I thought that's a charming fairy tale. Everyone wants to find a knight or royalty in his or her family tree. Ho-hum.

However, on the Gresham/Grissom/Grisham DNA results page, I discovered we matched their haplogroup: R1b (M343) western, southern and northern Europe, and pinpointing it further—1b2—England. We knew our immigrant ancestors migrated from County Kent in England. The twelve-marker results page did show a match, although not entirely, with one or two of the Grissom/Gresham men.

I upgraded my brother's test to 37 markers (another hundred bucks), and results showed up a few weeks later.

Excitement and anticipation grew to a fever pitch—and then plummeted.

The DNA match with Andrew Grisham—was **not** a match.

Some people had better luck with DNA testing.

What about DNA Results

Even with a close 37-marker match, which the DNA lab says gives a 90% chance of having a common ancestor within twelve generations, the relationship is distant **unless you have the same surname.**

We had a 37-marker match with another participant who had a different surname. I contacted the man. We can find no paper trail that could connect within twelve generations. His family did not even live in the same area of the United States within the twelve generations. We have found no explanation for the match.

Another friend confided her brother took the test. More than fifty men with the same surname separated into five or six groups with matches to each other, but none matched her brother.

So, we agree DNA tests are interesting, but maybe not yet accurate enough to prove the exact generation in the family tree and have not been at all helpful to us.

TRUE STORY: Joan Case of Manti, Utah, said she had been bouncing against a brick wall for several years trying to learn the name of her grandfather's father. She knew her grandfather Billy Thurman married a Creek Indian girl named China Perryman back in the 1880s. Billy Thurman and China had two children, Silas (Joan's father) and his sister Alice. When the children were very young, their mother died. The children were taken in and raised by China's family as members of the Creek tribe.

Although Billy Thurman came to visit occasionally, Silas and Alice knew little about their father or his background. The children lived with different members of their mother's family. When Silas became a teenager, he lived with his uncle, Legus Perryman, then chief of the Creek Nation. Billy Thurman died when Silas was still a young man.

Silas married late in life and fathered Joan when he was past forty. When Joan became curious about her genealogy, Silas had to think back many years to remember what little his father had told him about the Thurmans. The brick wall seemed insurmountable.

Along came DNA, and Joan's brother did the test. When the results came back, Joan's brother's DNA matched closely with another family named Thurman in Indiana. Joan contacted those people, and they were able to share enough information to know they had the same great grandfather, Isham Thurman, born about 1800. Joan found Isham listed in the 1850 census, living in Indiana with a son named Billy.

Thanks to DNA, Joan had reduced her brick wall to a small pile of rocks.

How About the Ladies, Bless Them?

Notice that Y-DNA, which is passed down solely from father to son, can connect to common ancestors. What do we know about maternal lines? Mitochondrial DNA (mtDNA), passed down from mother to both daughters and sons, changes much more slowly than Y-DNA, making it less useful for genealogical applications. What sets mtDNA apart is that unlike nuclear DNA, which you inherit equally from both father and mother, mtDNA is inherited from the mother only. All our mitochondria descend from those in our mother's egg cells.

If you are female and want to trace your mother's maiden name ancestry, you must locate her brother or father or a nephew with that surname. The test only looks at your female-inherited mitochondrial DNA.

Because mtDNA passes from a mother to her children with no input from any spouses along the way, this test only looks at the direct maternal line. Both men and women may take this test. It traces the direct maternal line without influence from other lines. According to a recent paper published on the subject, this mtDNA sequence analysis performs as a valuable tool to determine if individuals are biologically related through their mother's side of the family. This analysis is commonly referred to as a maternal lineage test.

An mtDNA maternal lineage test works by comparing the mitochondrial DNA (mtDNA) sequences of two or more individuals. People who are biologically related in this way will have similar mtDNA sequences, while individuals who are not biologically related will have dissimilar mtDNA sequences.

I think we need to give DNA testing a little more time to fully appreciate its usefulness in genealogy. However, the courts are using it successfully in prosecuting some hard-to-resolve court cases, and it is proving successful in finding birth families in adoptive situations.

In Summary:
- ✓ DNA testing can determine if two people are related or if two people descend from the same ancestor.
- ✓ Y-DNA testing relies on unbroken male lineages.
- ✓ Mitochondrial DNA (mtDNA) passes from mother to child.

CHAPTER NINETEEN

The Dating (and Calendar) Game

Preparing a timeline

When you hit a brick wall in your research, try setting up a timeline, and you may find yourself vaulting right over that wall. There are even software programs that will create a timeline for you. Inserting historical events will help you find your family's place in world history.

Timelines for individuals and families place events in a chronological format. Such a list will give you a great view of how your family fits and pits your historical research into perspective. By lining up the various events and dates in your family tree chronologically, you can get a look at the flow of the past. Imagining your ancestors participating in or observing these events takes you beyond names, dates, and locations to reach the "big picture" of circumstances that impacted them.

Preparing a simple timeline can help you discover other avenues for research. Here is a timeline example:

Chronology for Cornelius Cozine

1719: Born in English-held New York.
1732: Benjamin Franklin publishes *Poor Richard's Almanac*.
1737: CC in Capt. Joseph Robinson's co. of foot soldiers, NY.
1743: Married at Bushwyck, Long Island, NY, to Antje Staats.
1753: Cozine sold farmland in Brooklyn to Abraham Bogert.

1754:   At Haverstraw, Rockland Co, NY, visiting relatives.
1754:   French & Indian War begins.
1756:   Migration to the Jerseys, ca 1754-1757.
1758:   Raritan Church, NJ; Cornelius Kozyn[sic] elected deacon.
1759:   Cornelius Kozyn[sic] voted assistant of the Raritan ch.
1762:   Cornelius Kozyn[sic] elder, named to advise the pastor.
1763:   French & Indian War ends, the French are defeated.
1763:   Frans Cusaart named elder over Cornelius Kozyn[sic].
1765:   England places high taxes on sugar, Colonists protest
1765:   Stamp Act repealed.
1765:   Conewago Colony started east Gettysburg, York Co, PA.
1767:   Cornelius Cosyn's[sic] term as elder expired in NJ, 20 Mar
1768:   Cosyn inventories the estate of Pieter VanNest in N.J.
1768:   Wife Antje Staats buried at Readington church? (no proof)
1768:   Sold Somerset Co, NJ, farm to Hendrick Vanseveer.
1768:   100 families migrate from NJ to PA, Cozine too?
1768:   Indians burned houses at Conewago.
1769:   Some Low Dutch moved to Berkeley Co, VA.
1769:   Cosine [sic] purchased a 393-acre farm at Conewago.
1770:   Boston Massacre. Cozine becomes a Domine.
1772:   Baptisms by Domine Cozine recorded at Conewago.
1773:   Cozine married 2nd to Mary (Koning), widow VanOrden
1773:   Boston Tea Party.
1773:   Leah Demaree says Rev. Cozine is in NJ.
1775:   Fighting begins at Lexington and Concord.
1776:   Declaration of Independence, Rev. War begins.
1776:   Cosine [sic] listed as Sgt in Capt. Hugh Campbell's Co.
1778:   Raritan church burned by the British.
1779:   PA, Return of Taxables, Rev. Crozine [sic] & son listed.
1780s: Rev. Cosine commutes between Conowago & Berkeley
1781:   Member 5th class Inhabitants of Straban Twp, Fed. Army.
1781:   British surrender at Yorktown. The war ends.
1781:   The first Low Dutch emigration begins to KY.
1783:   Rev. Cozine taxed in Straban Twp, York Co PA.
1784:   Cozine is listed as Dominee of Conewago.
1784:   Capt. John Bodine's Co, York Co Militia, lists both Pvt 1784: 5th class Cornelius Cousine [sic] and his son, Cornelius Jr.
1786:   Rev. Cozine's will probated 30 Aug 1786, York Co PA.

1787:   Son, Cornelius Jr., dies in KY, a trust set up for his children.

How did that help?

Preparing this timeline allowed us to compare event dates. This comparison reveals reasons for us to believe both men, the Reverend Cornelius Cozine and his son, also called Cornelius Cozine, served in the militia during the Revolutionary period. The DAR accepted this preponderance of evidence.

The timeline also facilitated separating to which man the will and settlements referred, as well as determining migration dates. The father died in 1786 in Pennsylvania, and his estate was still in legal proceedings when the son died in Kentucky the next year. Both men had trusts set up for the younger man's children.

Let's Talk About Dates—Old Style and New Style

While on the subject of dates, you need to know what happened on 14 September 1752.

If you see a date written as 2 March 1735/6 you might think it means the year is uncertain even though the month and day are known. Wrong! This way of writing a date has a special meaning that all historians need to know more about.

Great Britain's Parliament passed an act in 1751, changing the country's dating system from the Julian calendar to the Gregorian. Before that, March served as the first month of the year. The new calendar designated January 1 to begin the New Year. On September 14, 1752, Great Britain, including the colonies, began to use the Gregorian calendar.

They removed eleven days from the year between the second and fourteenth days of September 1751. In theory, you should not find any English documents dated 3 to 13 September 1751.

Old Calendar, before 1752

    March   1st month of the year
    April   2nd month of the year
    May   3rd month of the year
    June   4th month of the year

July	5th month of the year
August	6th month of the year
September	7th month (also: 7ber, 7br, or VII-ber)
October	8th month (also: 8ber, 8br, or VIII-ber)
November	9th month (also called 9ber, 9br, or IX-ber)
December	10th month (also 10-ber, 10br, or Xber)
January	11th month of the year
February	12th month of the year

Goodbye Happy New Year in March

The previous calendar had its new year begin on March 25th. After 1752, any dates falling in from January 1st through March 24th had to show both the old year and the new one. For example, you would write 2/3/1718 as Feb. 3, 1718/9. January 22, 1720, would be 22 January 1720/1.

Most of the old dates in scholarly sources use this double dating, but many personal websites choose to show only one or the other of the years. Most genealogy programs only accept the four-number year. On many vital records with dates before 1752, you may find them a year off.

Example: The will of Thomas Branch, Senior, of Henrico County, VA, dated 25th, 8br 1688.

Translation. October 25, 1688, is not shown as 1688/9 because those double year dates are only needed from January through March.

Example: Thomas Jefferson, born in Virginia when it was a colony of Great Britain, died in Virginia long after the Revolution. See how they inscribed the dates on his tombstone at Monticello below his epitaph.

Born April 2, 1743 [Julian Calendar] O.S. Died July 4, 1826 [13 Apr 1743 Gregorian Calendar]

In Great Britain and countries of the British Empire, old-style or O.S. after a date means that the year is in the Julian calendar, in use in those countries until 1752. New style or N.S. means the date is in the Gregorian calendar, adopted on 14 September 1752 (new style).

In England and her territories, including the American colonies, both of these dating styles changed to modern usage in 1752. The phrases, old style and new style, are used to indicate whether dates were from the Julian calendar and Civil year (old style) or the Gregorian calendar and historical year (new style).

In other countries, the two elements changed at different times.

The Calendar and the Christian Church

Some groups say the calendar developed in the church of the second to fourth century for only two reasons. First, the new calendar emphasized Jewish religious holidays, and second, this new dating system gave an alternative to pagan festivities.

The Christian calendar was the universal calendar used for dating documents and setting work and school schedules in Europe until the modern era.

Most Christians are aware that the events in Jesus' life and ministry are not celebrated on the days they actually happened. Christmas was not a Christian holiday until the fourth century. The date of 25th December was fixed by the Council of Nicea to replace the pagan midwinter solstice festival of sol invictus (unconquered sun). December 25 also conveniently replaced the Roman winter festival of Saturnalia from December 17-21.

The Roman year was based on a complicated lunar calendar. The Roman civil year started on 1st January, and its use continued until the seventh century AD. The church generally wished to use one of its major festivals as the start of the year.

Christmas Day rather than 1 January started the new year for several centuries, from about AD 672 to the twelfth century.

Quaker Calendars

Another confusing dating situation concerns the unique way the Quakers dated events. They did not use names for days of the week or months of the year, because most of these names developed from the names of pagan gods.

A date such as August 19, 1748, will never be found in Quaker records. Instead, they would write, "19th da. 6th mo. 1748." You may also find this written as 6mo 19da 1748.

Why would they call it the sixth month since August is the eighth month? The Quakers, along with everyone else in the American Colonies and England, did not begin using the Gregorian calendar until 1752.

If exact days, months, and years are wanted, you must use the old Quaker records with great caution. Remember that until 1752 the first month is March. Before 1752, the new year in England started on 25 March.

When they established the new year starting on 1 January, the terms "old style" and "new style" came into use when quoting dates. In England and her territories, including the American colonies, both of these dating styles changed to modern usage in 1752. The phrases, old style and new style, are used to indicate whether dates were from the Julian calendar and Civil year (old style) or the Gregorian calendar and historical year (new style).

In other countries, the two elements changed at different times.

The Calendar and the Christian Church

Some groups say the calendar developed in the church during the second to fourth century for only two reasons.

First, the new calendar emphasized Jewish religious holidays.

Second, this new dating system gave an alternative to pagan festivities.

The Christian calendar was the universal calendar used for dating documents and setting work and school schedules in Europe until the modern era.

Most Christians are aware they celebrate the events in Jesus' life and ministry on days the Council of Nicea selected. Christmas was not a Christian holiday until the fourth century. The Council fixed the date of 25 December to replace the pagan midwinter solstice festival of sol Invictus (unconquered sun), and the Roman winter festival of Saturnalia from December 17-21.

The Roman Calendar

The Romans based their year on a complicated lunar calendar. The Roman civil year started on 1st January, and its use continued until the seventh century AD, now often referred to as CE, the Christian Era. The church wanted one of its major festivals at the start of the year. Christmas Day rather than 1 January started the new year for several centuries, from about AD 672 to the twelfth century.

In Summary

- ✓ Timelines are helpful, especially when family dates compare to world events.
- ✓ Our calendars changed in 1752 from Julian to Gregorian, moving New Year's Day from March 25 to January 1.
- ✓ Those dates affected by the calendar change you will find written with a slash as January 22, 1720/1, or 22 January 1753 NS (new-style).
- ✓ Double year dates are needed from January through March 1752.
- ✓ OS (old-style) and NS (new-style) are used to indicate Julian Calendar (OS) or Gregorian Calendar (NS).
- ✓ Quaker records used numbers rather than names for days of week and months of each year.

CHAPTER TWENTY

Getting it in print

Are we done yet?

If you are unable to continue the work, what will happen to your material? When Mom dies, and the kids empty the house, most genealogy and family history papers go to the dump. The ONLY way to prevent this is for you, the one who collected all this genealogy and family history – to do something permanent with it. Do you have any family members who share your interest and would want to carry on with your effort? Decide what person or organization might accept your files and other materials. Ask if they would want to preserve it after you are gone. Many libraries and archives are under a crunch for space and may not accept every donation.

Why Not a Special Repository

If you have several persons working on a particular ancestral name or ethnic group, you may want to see about setting up an appropriate repository at a specific library to preserve all that history.

As part of a large group of descendants of Low Dutch (Holland) ancestry whose members settled for a generation in Mercer County, Kentucky, we contacted the Historical Research Library in the county seat town about our wishes. They applied and were approved for a grant to set up the repository and hire a librarian dedicated to that collection for our Low Dutch history.

Preserve your work by publishing

The task of publishing a book may seem overwhelming, but there are ways to take it in small bites.

Your goal is to get your information published so no one else will have to reinvent the wheel.

Writing a book is a lot of work. Getting a publisher to read your tome is even more so, although family history books seem to increase in value each year when sold on e-bay.

You need to be sure of your goal when you start and decide how much you are willing to give of yourself.

Here are some choices:
- Self-publish
- Assisted self-publishing
- Submitting to a small publisher
- Submitting to a well-known publisher
- Hiring a vanity publisher

No matter who publishes your book, you will be the one responsible for creating the demand. Books do not sell just by sitting on a shelf. If profit is a motive, you must treat the venture as a business. One writing website claims from start to finish, writers will spend ten percent of their time writing the book, fifteen percent publishing it, and seventy-five percent on marketing and promoting the finished product. I'd recommend making it more fifty/fifty; fifty percent each on writing and marketing.

Self-publishing

Do a little market study. Beyond friends and family, who will want to buy your book? Knowing how to reach those people is something you need to know before investing in self-publishing. This knowledge would also help you sell the manuscript to a publisher.

Share your manuscript with members of your target audience and ask them for an honest assessment. Submit an excerpt to a magazine or newspaper on speculation to see what interest is out there. If you find an audience, print a few books and promote them locally to see how they sell. If they do not sell, you have not lost much. You may want to try a print-on-demand option. Once the printer receives and processes the files, they put the book out for sale through their distribution channels. Then you do not fill your garage full of books.

Develop a solid marketing plan to get an accurate estimate of how many books may sell. Most self-publishers initially print 500 to 3,000 copies. Family historians usually publish fewer than 300 copies and the fewer you reproduce, the more it costs per book. If profit is your motive, the initial cost of producing and printing fewer than five hundred copies may be higher than you anticipate. You must decide how many unsold books you want to store in your garage. The harsh truth is that 95% of all books published sell fewer than 7,500 copies; family history books average hundreds less than that.

With self-publishing, you are the publisher. You buy the paper, hire an editor, illustrator, and a proofreader, learn to do page layout and design. As an alternative, you could put out the money to hire a book designer, printer, collator, and binder. There are many decisions to make about the cover, and all are price-related: one-color, two-color, four-color, full-color, hardback, softcover. Conclude whether to hire an artist or design it yourself. You must decide the size of the finished product and how you want it bound. If you feel comfortable with all that and can afford the expense if it does not sell, go for it.

There are other good reasons to self-publish. You will learn about the arts and crafts associated with the business. You will never again look at any published book in the same way.

When You Should Self-Publish

There are two situations when self-publishing or assisted publishing is not only suggested but highly recommended:

You are a speaker or teacher and need the book for classes or workshops you will be leading.

You don't care about the money and wish to have a book to give away that contains family history, memoirs, unpublished poetry, or some other unique information.

How Much Will It Cost?

There is no typical price or method to self-publish because there are so many options. Will you require acid-free paper for printing? Do you want it in hardback or leather-bound? Do you want offset printing or high-speed copying? How many copies do you need, or can you sell?

First Things First

If you decide to self-publish, you will be in good company. Walt Whitman, William Blake, Benjamin Franklin, Gertrude Stein, D.H. Lawrence, James Joyce, and Mark Twain all got started that way. Sometimes people self-publish because they think they will make a lot of money. Publishers like to make money too, so if you are not able to convince a publisher to market your book, that is probably not a good sign.

Remember, out of every ten books published, three earn a profit, four recover costs, and the rest lose money. How do publishers stay in business? Why do writers keep writing? Because of the dream.

Before you start writing, read the classic book, *The Elements of Style,* by Strunk and White (The Little Book). No one ever summed up the rules of good writing better.

Preliminaries

If you decide to self-publish, here are some preliminary activities.
- Protect your copyright.
- Secure a Library of Congress number.
- Get a Cataloging in Publication (CIP) number.

- Request an International Standard Business Number (ISBN).
- Get your title listed in *Books in Print*.

Assisted Self-Publishing

You may want to print a project that is too expensive for either a commercial or small press. If you have the money and the audience, you may wish to commit your funds to bring your work before the public. There are many options and methods to accomplish this, from using the local copy shop to hiring a printing press.

Usually, the best way to get your family history in print quickly is to choose self-publishing or assisted publishing. These are two similar but different methods. The advantage of this type of publishing is you get to keep all the profit instead of splitting it with a publishing company. The disadvantage is there is rarely any profit in publishing family history.

Assisted publishing is more comfortable, but the upfront cost is higher. With assisted self-publishing, the publishing house usually assigns you a mentor. You still have control of the finished product, and you have someone to hold your hand while you make those tough decisions about paper, color, and layout. Assisted publishing is quite a time-consuming project.

TRUE STORY: Several years ago, I had a friend named Jane, an excellent poet. She learned she had terminal cancer and wanted to have her poetry published before she died. Finding a royalty publisher who wants to publish a poetry book may not be impossible, but it is highly unlikely unless you are already famous. Most poets self-publish or use a so-called vanity press. Jane asked me to help her. I knew how to publish newspapers but did not have a clue about publishing books. She said, "*Then we will learn together,*" and we did. My friend lived to see her book published and was able to give poetry readings before her time ran out. She never sold many copies. Her family tells me they still have books stored in the garage a dozen years later, but making money was not her goal. Jane's book lives on. I always enjoy reading it, and I hear her voice with every poem I read, just as her family does. That money was a substantial investment for her purposes.

Vanity Publishing

Some people think self-publishing is akin to vanity publishing, but the two are worlds apart. Vanity publishing is somewhat of a deception, although they do fill a need in the world. Vanity press publishers pretend that among all the manuscripts submitted they chose your book. Vanity presses are like retail stores—they will serve any customer who has the money to pay them. A vanity press, sometimes also called a subsidy press, promises to promote your book—they can justify a higher price that way—but promotion is still up to you.

Most book reviewers and bookstores shun vanity titles. A vanity press promises many things, but little is delivered. The author pays them to publish the book and receives only a royalty from books sold. If you decide to go this way, remember *caveat emptor*. Let the buyer beware. Check out your options and be sure that is the best solution for you.

Do it Yourself – With a Little bit of Help

You might want to check out Amazon publishing, a subsidiary of Amazon.com. Once you are satisfied the manuscript is perfect, and your proofreader agrees you upload the digital copy of your .pdf document to KDP.com. The program converts your uploaded file to a print-ready book. They may reject it for any number of reasons; for instance, if the process reveals any illustrations are not at least 300 dpi (dots per inch), or the file is corrupt.

Your uploaded file is displayed online in a virtual version of your printed book, so you can preview end-to-end, allowing you to spot and repair the highlighted problems quickly. Tools like Interior Reviewer and Cover Creator enable you to do-it-yourself easily. There are no upfront costs and no need to carry inventory. Amazon handles manufacturing and shipping. Your book remains in-stock, without inventory, made on-demand when customers order.

If Amazon accepts your work, you can order a proof copy (called an Advance Reader Copy or ARC) that you receive in a week or so. If you are satisfied with the proof, just give Amazon the go-ahead to put it on the market, and order as many copies as you want to sell yourself. Amazon.com will be selling copies also and will send you royalties.

I'm sure you can find other programs like this, but I published a color travel book on Amazon.com and am pretty happy with how it came out.

Try Submitting It First

My suggestion to those who want to get their book published is to try the commercial market first. Many small presses who may be interested in publishing your work if your manuscript is well presented and would be stimulating to many people.

This suggestion is especially useful if you want to fictionalize your family history into novel form, as is quite popular now, or write it as a memoir.

No one enjoys receiving a rejection slip, but you do learn a little more with each one. Study your *Writers Market* book, find a publisher who publishes the kind of books you write, and follow instructions. You must be patient because publishing houses usually hold those manuscripts at least two or three months. You should probably allow at least a year to market your script.

Here is a typical timeline for most:
- Write the manuscript—nine to eighteen months.
- Write the proposal—six months.
- Locate and sign with an agent—three months (or longer).
- Sell the book to a publisher—one to four months.

- Book in hand—nine to twelve months or longer after acceptance.

Submitting to a Large Publishing House

Few **full-service** publishers accept family history manuscripts unless you are from a famous family like the Kennedys, have been elected president, or were born Prince William.

Perhaps you have an unusual ethnic background like Alex Haley, author of *Roots,* in 1976 based on his African ancestors. The book followed several generations in the lives of a slave family. The twelve-hour TV mini-series based on Haley's best-selling novel *Roots* held the single-episode rating record for many years and stirred a new interest in genealogy.

Maybe you could match the memoir, *Angela's Ashes,* by Irish author Frank McCourt. McCourt's bestselling novel tells the story of his poverty-stricken childhood in Brooklyn and Ireland. The book, published in 1996, won the Pulitzer Prize for biography or autobiography. Paramount Pictures released the memoir as a feature film in 1999, and it became an international success. "Worse than the ordinary miserable childhood is the miserable Irish childhood," writes Frank McCourt in *Angela's Ashes.* "Worse yet is the miserable Irish Catholic childhood." The son of a chronically unemployed and nearly unemployable alcoholic father described his "miserable childhood." Mix in abject poverty, frequent untimely deaths, and critical illnesses; you have a difficult early life. Fortunately, in McCourt's able hands, this formula also carried all the makings for a compelling memoir.

Can you come up with a formula like that?
In that case—Wow! Go for it!

Your Elevator Pitch

Your book has to be different from all the others to be successful. You must present some unusual twists to get the attention of agents and editors. They need that information to pitch it to the booksellers and book buyers. Pretend you are about to appear on a national TV show to talk about your book and describe it in not more than three sentences. Make it a 30-second sales pitch. You should use this quick pitch every time some agent, publisher, or another writer asks what you are writing, even in an elevator.

Here are a couple of books that can help you in writing your best-selling family history. Sharon DeBartolo Carmack's, *You Can Write Your Family History,* and M. Carolyn Steele's *Preserving Family Legends for Future Generations* are terrific guides. (See bibliography for full information.)

Even if a publisher accepts your work, the ugly truth is full-service publishers do things authors don't like. You are selling them your manuscript, and you must turn loose of it. They may change titles, design ugly unreadable jackets, write boring jacket text, fail to get books distributed, and print too few copies. Rarely would you have any input into the cover design or layout of your book, how many copies produced, or where and how marketed. Usually, you even have to buy copies of your book from the publisher if you want to have some on hand.

You may be able to avoid some of these problems by going to a small publisher.

Small Publishing Houses

Small publishing companies pay you rather than your money going for the product. Small publishers are more willing to work with an author to produce the book the author wants. They work harder to create one you will be able to sell to your market, thereby making money for both of you. A small publisher can usually produce the finished product quicker than a large press, and the book stays on the market longer. Ask other authors to recommend a good company.

How Much Can You Make

When you self-publish or use assisted self-publishing, you do not receive an advance and royalty is questionable. You publish your work, and you keep one hundred percent of the profit.

If a publisher buys your manuscript, you may receive an advance on their expected profits. After they recoup your advance, you may receive a royalty. The best you can hope for is about fifteen percent of the selling price. Often it is more like six percent. Books that don't sell quickly take a long time, if ever, to see any royalties.

Small publishers handle royalties in different ways. Some pay advances, some do not, but you are not paying them to publish it.

Don't quit your day job even if the publisher wants to buy your proposal. A rare person makes a living by doing nothing but writing books. As part of your market research, browse through your favorite bookstore in the section where your book will fit when published. Most of these authors are professors, journalists, therapists, celebrities, or professional speakers actively engaged in whatever genre they choose.

What Is the Truth About Copyright?

Most beginning writers worry about someone stealing their work. You have a copyright the moment you put your manuscript in written form or on tape. You do have to prove it is your original work, and the date you created it in case anyone challenges your copyright. The best way is to register your copyright with the U.S. Copyright Office in Washington DC, but there are other methods.

No publication or registration or other action in the copyright office is required to secure copyright. There are, however, certain definite advantages to registration. Go to the webpage:
http://www.copyright.gov/.

The use of the copyright notice is the responsibility of the copyright owner and does not require advance permission from, or registration with, the copyright office.

Congress passed the first copyright protection law in 1790. A revision of that law in 1909 granted copyright for 28 years with the option of renewing for another 20 years. The most recent change of that law became effective in 1978. Today's copyright gives protection for the life of the author plus at least fifty years after their death.

This Copyright Act of 1976 took effect in 1978 and added security by copyright before publication.

The magic elements of the copyright notice are:

1. The use of the word "Copyright" or the symbol ©,
2. The year of first publication, and
3. The name of the owner of the copyright.

Example: © 2006 John Doe

Place this notice the copyright page, which follows the full title page. You must send two copies of the work to the U.S. Copyright Office for the Library of Congress within three months of publication. www.copyright.gov.

Registration of copyright may be taken care of at that time also. Complete a form available online at the copyright site and paying a fee.

Copyright registration

To register a work, send the following three elements in the same envelope or package to:
Library of Congress
Copyright Office
101 Independence Avenue SE
Washington, DC 20559-6000

Put into one envelope or package:
A completed application, mentioned earlier.
Payment to Register of Copyrights.
($45 check or money order.)

Nonreturnable copy(ies) of the material to be registered.

Your registration becomes effective on the day the copyright office receives your application, payment, and copy(ies) in acceptable form. If your submission is in order, you will receive a certificate of registration in about six months.

Library of Congress Number

A Library of Congress catalog card number is a unique identification number the Library of Congress assigns to the catalog record created for each book in its collection. The Library of Congress assigns this number while the book is being cataloged.

Under certain circumstances, a card number can be assigned before the book is published through the Preassigned Card Number Program. For more information, go to the Library of Congress website:
  http://www.loc.gov/index.html

CIP—Cataloging in Publication

A Cataloging in Publication record (a.k.a. CIP data) is a bibliographic record prepared by the Library of Congress for a book not yet been published. When the book is published, the publisher includes the CIP data on the copyright page, thereby facilitating book processing for libraries and book dealers.

ISBN—A Very Important Number

The International Standard Book Number (ISBN) is a 13-digit number that uniquely identifies books and book-like products published internationally. This is the number used by bookstores, libraries, distributors, and buyers to locate a particular book. Formerly the ISBNs were ten digits, but in 1996 they converted to thirteen, so don't publish the shorter numbers in your book.

Publishers can buy one or a block of ISBNs. The Library of Congress does not administer or distribute International Standard Book Numbers.

Contact *R.R. Bowker* at: 630 Central Avenue, New Providence, NJ 07974; Telephone: (877) 310-7333 Fax: (908) 665-2895; or on the website www.isbn.org/. Allow 15 business days for non-priority processing from the time an ISBN application is received at the agency.

R.R. Bowker is the ISBN agency in the United States, responsible for assigning ISBNs as well as providing information and advice on the uses of the ISBN system to publishers and the publishing industry in general.

R.R. Bowker is charged by the International ISBN Agency with the collection of bibliographic data on titles published in the United States. This title data is found in the databases of *Books in Print*. Book titles should be registered with *Books in Print* at www.bowkerlink.com

What Is Public Domain?

Any work created before September 1909 is now in public domain, no longer protected by copyright. It is fair game for anyone who wishes to publish it.

Some books published *after* September 1909 are also in public domain because their copyright was not renewed. If you find an old family history and update the book in some way to make it new again, you may be able to register a new copyright for the material. There is nothing illegal about that.

Summing It Up

If you decide to self-publish or go with assisted self-publishing, I recommend a very special book. I don't get a commission on the sale of this book and only met the authors once several years ago. *The Complete Guide to Self-Publishing, Everything you need to Know to Write, Publish, Promote and Sell Your Own Book,* by Marilyn Ross. Now in the 5th edition,

Complete Guide... will tell you all about how to format your manuscript.

Yes, writing a family history book is a lot of work, but when you hold the finished product in your hand, you have made your dream a reality. You have also bookmarked your family's place in history and left a legacy for future generations.

In Summary

- ✓ Study the market when you are ready to print.
- ✓ Decide your method of publishing:
- ✓ Self-publish
- ✓ Assisted self-publishing
- ✓ Submitting to a small publisher
- ✓ Submitting to a large publisher
- ✓ Paying a vanity publisher
- ✓ With conventional publishing allow at least a year from acceptance to printed copy in your hand.
- ✓ Marketing your book requires time and energy

Book Summary

Genealogy is an exciting and entertaining hobby. You begin by looking for family information "just for fun," and it turns into an adventure, with you playing the part of a private detective.

Identifying ancestors and sharing family history information can become one of the most important things you do in your life. Discovering where your family fits in history is one of the most extraordinary legacies you could leave to your descendants. The history of the world around them affected their lives and the choices they made.

The joy of the experience is challenging to describe to someone not involved in the practice. Researching is a great way to meet new people and find friends with the same interests.

While you are learning about the correct ways to research your family and the different sources available, you need to be aware of some research mistakes you do not want to make.

Skipping generations. For example, *"Someone said my ancestor descended from the third king of England, so I started tracing his family, but I am missing a few generations."* Those generations will probably remain missing. Always begin tracing your family with yourself and work your way back in time—not the opposite.

Believe what you find, with some exceptions. For example, someone found an abundance of information about her family genealogy. She refused to copy any of it because she was sure her ancestor "had not been married twice." It's easier to copy the information and check it out later than be unable to find it again.

Learn everything possible about a location before traveling there for research. You need to know precisely where to go, who you need to find, and the best time to be there.

Don't be surprised to find several generations with the same names. In our family, we boast five generations of Peter Branches; fathers and sons, nephews and cousins with the same name. Sometimes they are referred to as Junior or Senior, sometimes as "Peter the Younger." You never know which Peter Branch without double-checking dates.

Spelling is questionable. Keep an open mind about the spelling of your family names. Early spelling was phonetic. Word spellings most often are just an inconvenience, but changes in name spellings are much more significant. It is essential to be aware of different possible name spellings when you are researching so you don't overlook records that might refer to your family.

Also, don't believe everything you read. Genealogists are known for sharing information with other genealogists. Not all this information is reliable.

Published family histories are not all equal. Some are full of errors. Internet genealogy information cannot always be relied on unless the source can be verified. Never assume anything is correct without proof.

Acronyms and Abbreviations
Some of the most common terms used this book.
- Abt — About
- AC — Ancestor chart
- Aft — after
- Aka/a.k.a./AKA — Also known as
- Bef — before
- Ca — circa
- CD-ROM - Compact Disc-Read-Only-Memory
- CDV — Carte de Visite — Calling Card photograph
- CIP — Cataloging in Publication
- DAR — Daughters of American Revolution
- DUVCW — Daughters of Union Veterans of Civil War
- Est — estimated
- FGS — Family Group Sheet
- FHC — Family History Centers (LDS)
- GAR — Grand Army of the Republic (Union veterans of Civil War)
- Inst. — instant, same month
- ISBN — International Standard Book Number
- LDS — The Church of Jesus Christ of Latter Day Saints (Mormon)
- NACO — National Association of Counties
- NEHGS — New England Historic Genealogical Society
- PERSI — Periodical Source Index
- Pr — probably

- Ult — ultimate, previous month
- SAR — Sons of American Revolution
- SUVCW — Sons of Union Veterans of Civil War
- VA — Veterans Administration
- WPA — Work Progress Administration

Bibliography

I list here many writings that have been of use in the making of this book. The bibliography is by no means a complete record of all the works and sources consulted. It indicates the substance and range of reading upon which I have formed my idea and will serve as a convenience for those who wish to pursue the study of genealogy. I included ISBNs when known and other identifying data to help readers find the reference books they need.

Angevine, Erma. *Instructions for Beginners in Genealogy*. 3rd ed, rev; Arlington VA: Education Dept, National Genealogical Society, 1993.

Banta, Elsa M. *Banta Pioneers...* (1983) and *A Supplement to Banta Pioneers and records of the wives and allied families* (1985) 14 pp.; privately printed by E. M. Banta.

Carmack, Sharon DeBartolo. *You Can Write Your Family History*. Cincinnati, OH: Betterway Books, 2003; ISBN 1-55870-641-0, www.familytreemagazine.com.

Cerny, Johni & Eakle, Arlene (Editors). *The Source, A Guidebook of American Genealogy*. Salt Lake City, UT: Ancestry Publishing Co, 1984. ISBN 0-916489-00-0.

Cheney, Theodore A. Rees. *Writing Creative Non-Fiction, How to use fiction techniques to make your nonfiction more interesting, dramatic—and vivid*. Cincinnati, OH: Writers Digest Books, 1987 ISBN 0-89879-255-X.

Conley, Robyn. *Be Your Own Book Doctor, so you can cure what ails your writing.* TX: AWOC.com. 2003. ISBN 0-9707507-3-0.

Croom, Emily Anne. *Unpuzzling Your Past, A Basic Guide to Genealogy, 2nd Ed.* Cincinnati, OH: Betterway Publications, 182 pp. and (same title) 4th edition Betterway Books, 2001, 284 pp. ISBN 1-558700-5562.

Davidson, James West & Lytle, Mark Hamilton. *After the Fact, Vol I, the Art of Historical Detection, 1st ed.* New York: Alfred A. Knopf, 1982. ISBN 0-394-32129-4.

Eastman, Dick. *Eastman Online Genealogy Newsletter* (Sponsored by RootsBooks) Free.
http://blog.eogn.com/eastmans_online_genealogy/

Everton, George B Sr (Editor). *The Handy Book for Genealogists, 7th ed.* Logan, UT: The Everton Publishers, Inc. 1981.

Frensh, Christopher W. (Editor). *The Associated Press STYLEBOOK and Libel Manual*, Rev. Ed. Addison-Wesley Publishing Co, Inc, 1987. ISBN 0-201-10433-4.

Goldstein, Norm. *The Associated Press Stylebook.* Basic Books, Rev. ed. 2004. 378 pp. ISBN-13: 978-0465004881 (The Bible of the newspaper industry).

Greenwood, Val D. *The Researcher's Guide to American Genealogy.* Baltimore: Genealogical Publishing Co., 1973.

Harland, Derek. *Genealogical Research Standards.* Published by The Genealogical Society of The Church of Jesus Christ of Latter-day Saints. Salt Lake City, UT: Bookcraft Inc. 1963, 8th pr 1971.

Haley, Alex. *Roots, the Saga of An American Family*. New York: Doubleday. 1st edition 1976. 688 pp. ISBN-13 978-0385037877.

Hoffman, Marian (editor). *Genealogical and Local History Books in Print*. Baltimore, MD: Genealogical Publishing Co. 5th edition 1997. 550 pages, ISBN-13: 978-0806315355.

Kirkham, E. Kay. *The Handwriting of American Records for a Period of 300 Years*. Salt Lake City, UT: Everton Publishers, Inc, 1981.

Leonard, Carolyn B. (magazine article) "Wm S. Prettyman, Frontier Photographer." *Persimmon Hill*. Autumn 2006.

McCourt, Frank. *Angela's Ashes*. New York: Scribner, 1996. 368 pp, ISBN-13: 978-0684874357.

McCutcheon, Marc. *The Writers Guide to Everyday Life in the 1800s, for writers of historical fiction, westerns, romance, action adventure, thrillers and mysteries*. Writers Digest Books, 1993. ISBN 0-89879-541-9.

Mills, Elizabeth Shown. *Evidence, Citation and Analysis for the Family Historian*. Baltimore: Genealogical Publishing Company, 1997; and *Evidence Explained: Citing History Sources from Artifacts to Cyberspace*, 885 pp, Genealogical Publishing Co, 2007. ISBN 0-80631-781-7.

Moorshead, Halvor. *Dating Old Photographs,* and *More Dating Old Photographs*. Family Chronicle, 2000.

Polking, Kirk & Meranus, Leonard S. (Editors); *Law and the Writer, Updated copyright law edition*. Writers Digest Books, 1981. ISBN 0-89879-009-3.

Ritchie, Donald A. *Doing Oral History: A practical guide, 2nd Edition.* New York: Twayne Publishers. Toronto: Maxwell Macmillan. New York: Maxwell Macmillan International, 2005. ISBN 0-19-515434-7. 265 pages.

Roorbach, Bill. *Writing Life Stories, How to Make Memories into Memoirs, Ideas into Essays, and Life into Literature.* Cincinnati, OH: Story Press, 1998. ISBN 1-884910-36-X.

Rose, Christine & Ingalls, Kay Germain. *The Complete Idiot's Guide to Genealogy.* Alpha books, a Division of Macmillan Reference USA, Simon & Schuster Macmillan Co, 1633 Broadway, NY, 1997, ISBN 0-02-861947-1.

Roskey, William A. *How to Trace Your Family Tree.* American Genealogical Research Institute Staff. New York: Dolphin Books, Doubleday & Co, 1975. ISBN 0-385-09885-5.

Ross, Tom & Marilyn. *The Complete Guide to Self Publishing, Everything You Need to Know to Write, Publish, Promote and Sell Your Own Book*, 3rd Edition. Cincinnati, OH: Writers Digest Books, 1994; ISBN 0-89879-646-6

Shaw, Eva. *Writing the Nonfiction Book.* Loveland, CO: Rodgers & Nelsen, 1999. ISBN 0-9662696-2-4.

Sperry, Kip. *Reading Early American Handwriting.* Baltimore, MD: Genealogical Publishing Company; 1998.

Steele, M. Carolyn. *Preserving Family Legends for Future Generations.* Paperback. Denton, TX: Roots and Branches 2008; 136 pp; ISBN-13: 978-0937660157.

Strunk, William & White, E.B. *The Elements of Style*; 7th edition, Filiquarian Publishing LLC, 2007. ISBN 1-59986-933-0.

The Battle Abbey Roll with some account of the Norman Lineages, by the Duchess of Cleveland. published 1848, reprinted 2008. Baltimore MD: Genealogical.com, 120 pp; ISBN: 9780806308074; available online at http://books.google.com.

The Norman People and Their Existing Descendants in the British Dominions and the United States of America. 500 pp hardcover 1st pub London: Henry S. King & Co, 1874, reprinted 1999, Baltimore, MD: Genealogical Publishing Company ISBN-13: 978-0806306360;
available online at http://books.google.com.

University of Chicago Press Staff (editor). *The Chicago Manual of Style*. Ill: University of Chicago Press, 15th edition 2003; 984 pages; ISBN-13: 978-0226104034.

Welling, William. *Collector's Guide to Nineteenth Century Photographs*. New York: Collier Books, a Division of Macmillan Publishers, 1976.

Zinsser, William. *On Writing Well: An Informal Guide to Writing Nonfiction* 2nd ed. New York: Harper & Row publishers, 1980.

WWW.ANCESTRY.COM
You can sign up for a 14-day free trial of this world's largest family history website; you have to give a credit card number, but they don't charge your card for two weeks. By that time, they expect you will be hooked!

WWW.CYNDISLIST.COM
Cyndi's List of Genealogy Sites on the Internet; here you will find a large categorized and cross-referenced directory of sites useful for genealogical research, with hundreds of thousands of links.

WWW.HERITAGEQUEST.COM
(now Pro-Quest) combines digital, searchable images of U.S. Federal census records with the digitized version. From the

1790 - 1930 U.S. federal censuses. It offers more than 20,000 book titles, including nearly 8,000 family histories and over 12,000 local histories. Additionally, there are more than 250 primary-source documents such as tax lists, city directories, probate records, and more.

WWW.FOOTNOTE.COM

At Footnote.com you'll be able to view, save, and share original images of historical documents from American history, including pension and service records of the American Revolution. Footnote.com collections feature documents relating to the Revolutionary War, Civil War, WWI, WWII, U.S. Presidents, historical newspapers, naturalization documents, and much more. Some other very notable material includes the Matthew Brady collection of Civil War photos and UFO documents from 1947 to 1969. Libraries subscribing to Footnote.com will be able to provide remote access to patrons.

There are too many great databases online for me to list them all. Find them on Cyndi's List, above.

Alphabetical index

2

20/20 Method 49

A

Acronyms and Abbreviations . 246
Adams, Abigail Smith 32
Adams, John Quincy 32
Alexander the Great 182
Allen County Public Library 186
ambrotype 59
Ancestor Chart 2
Ancestral Quest 147
Ancestry.com 76, 148, 150
Apple computer genealogy
   software 146
Assisted Self Publishing 235

B

Baker, John 99
Banta, Elsa M. 192
birth certificates 80
Blake, William 234
Bodine, John 224
Bogert, Abraham 223
Bounty Land 197, 200
Branch, Addie M. 39
Branch, Alpha C. 39
Branch, Ida Elizabeth 108
Branch, Joseph 91, 92
Branch, Levi 107, 108
Branch, Mary E. 37
Branch, Samuel 178
Branch, Samuel C. 112
Branch, Thomas 226
Brocum, William 181

C

calendar, old style . 226, 227, 228, 229
calendar, Quaker 227
Campbell, Hugh 224

carbon paper 46, 47
Carmack, Sharon DeBartolo ... 239
Carnegie, Andrew 183
Carow, Edith Kermit 206
Carte de Visite 61
census taker 36, 38, 39, 41, 42, 48, 102
Civil War veteran 205, 209
Clark, Samuel 181
Coat of Arms 81, 82
collateral relationships 6, 10
Color Coding Files 88
Confederate 1, 201, 202, 204
Continentals 198
County Clerk 153, 157, 158
County Treasurer 153, 157
Court Clerk 153, 157, 165, 171
Cozine, George A. 170
Cozine, Rev. Cornelius 181
Cozine, Thomas H. B. 97
Craig, Mary 170, 171
Curtis, Edward S. 62
Cyndi's List 93, 110, 148, 150, 195, 251

D

daguerreotype 59
Daguerreotype 59
DAR Library 185
DAR Patriot Index 198
de Braunche, Peter 101
de Braunche, Roger 101, 218
death certificates 80
deeds, types of 161, 162
Demaree, Leah 224
Dick, Albert B. 47
DNA, Mitochondrial 221
DNA, Y chromosome 217, 218
Dollarhide, William 194
Dudrey, Abraham V. 207
Dudrey, William 207, 208, 209

253

E

Eastman, Dick 119, 147
estates 164, 165, 169
Eversharp 44

F

Faber, Eberhard 44
Family Group Sheet 6
Family Tree Maker 146
Familysearch.org 151
Farthing, Hamilton 167
Fausset, Robert 115
Feather, RBR 208
Ferneau, Vesther.... 135, 137, 139
fieldstones 134
flu epidemic 122
Footnote.com 151, 200
Franklin, Benjamin 223, 234

G

Generations Family Tree 147
Geocaching 111
George Washington 29, 40, 96
Godey's Lady's Book 65
GPS 110, 111
Grantee 159, 160, 163
Grantor 159, 160, 163
Gregorian calendar 225, 226, 227, 229
Grisham, Andrew 218, 219
Gritton, F. N. 171
Guardianship 166, 169
Gutenberg 182

H

Haley, Alex 238
Haloid Company 47
hand marks 163
Handy Book 78, 153, 154, 155
Harvard, John 183
Hawkins, Isaac 43
Heritage Quest 103, 150, 188
Houston, Sam. 135, 136, 137, 139

I

Indianapolis 115
Indians not taxed 43
ink recipe 43
intestate 165
ISBN 242

J

Jefferson, Thomas 43, 183
Jones, Jerry 149
Jones, Sarah "Sally" 133
Joyce, James 234
Julian calendar 225
Julius Caesar 182

K

Key, David 100
Kirkham, E. Kay 56

L

Land records 158
Large, Solomon 103
Large, Thomas 103
Lawrence, D.H. 234
LDS Family History Library 184
Legacy Family Tree 146
libraries, circulating 183
libraries, collecting 183
Library of Congress 183, 185, 188, 234, 241, 242, 243
Loyalists 198

M

Mailing Lists Online 93
Marriage bonds 169
McCourt, Frank 238
Miller's Law 31
Mimeograph 47
Moorshead, Halvor 66
Moorshead, Valvor 249
Morlan, John 178

N

National Archives 36, 186, 199, 200, 201, 204
National Association of Counties 5
New England Historic Genealogical Society 186

O

Old Soldiers' Home 207

P

Patronymics 99
PC genealogy software ... 146, 147
pensions 199, 201, 204, 205
Perryman, China 220
Personal Ancestral File (PAF) .. 147
Pottawatomi 40
Primary Sources 76
Probate 165
Probate Court 165

Q

Query Letter 94

R

R.R. Bowker 243
Registrar of Deeds 157
Research Log 75, 77
Robinson, Joseph 223
Roosevelt, Alice 206
Roosevelt, Archibald 206
Roosevelt, Kermit 206
Roosevelt, Quentin 206
Roosevelt, Theodore 205
Roots Magic 147
RootsWeb Surname List 149
Ross, Marilyn 243

S

Samuel Branch 22, 171
Scott, Lamyh Ann 178
Secondary sources 76

self-publishing 232, 233, 235, 236, 243, 244
Smith, Adonijah 96
Smith, Furman 96
Smith, John Axford 96
Smith, Mary 96, 136, 138
Smith, Stephen 96
Smith, William 96
Soundex 36
Soundex coding 102
sources . vii, 1, 5, 7, 32, 77, 79, 95, 99, 103, 148, 177, 183, 193, 195, 197, 226, 245
Sperry, Kip 56
Staats, Antje 224
Stedman, Alexander 81, 133
Steele, M. Carolyn 239
Stein, Gertrude 234
Stewart, Anna 115
Stribling, Bradford S. 167
Stribling, Elizabeth Williams ... 167
Stribling, Mahala C. 167
Stribling, Margaret E. 167
Stribling, Mary Ann 167
Surrogate Court 165

T

testate 165
Thorndale, William 194
Thurman, Billy 220
tintype 59
Twain, Mark 234

U

U.S. Geological Survey 111, 193
U.S. marshal 41
Union soldier 201
Union veteran 205

V

Van Nest, Pieter 224
Van Wyck, Abram 99
Vanarsdale 101
vanity press 235, 236

Vanity Publishing..................... 236
Vanseveer, Hendrick 224
vital records 78, 80, 226

W

Waterman, L. E......................... 44
websites (genealogy) 251, 252

Whitman, Walt........................ 234
Williams, Benjamin W. 167
Woodmen of the World . 127, 130

X

Xerox Company 47

Index of Illustrations

FIGURE 1: GENEALOGY IS LIKE A BOX OF CHOCOLATES. v
FIGURE 2: FIGURE 1: A SIMPLE ANCESTOR CHART (AC) 3
FIGURE 3: A SIMPLE FAMILY GROUP SHEET (FGS) 6
FIGURE 4: NINA CROSLEY COZINE'S FAMILY BIBLE. 8
FIGURE 5: THE SAMUEL C. BRANCH FAMILY ABOUT 1875. 20
FIGURE 6: FAMILY MYSTERY RELATIONSHIP SOLVED. 21
FIGURE 9: SAM'L C. BRANCH 23
FIGURE 9: CAROLINE STRIBLING BRANCH 23
FIGURE 9: STEPHEN S. BRANCH (1835-1911) 23
FIGURE 10: JOHN & ABIGAIL ADAMS—APPARENTLY NOT MY COUSINS AFTER ALL. 32
FIGURE 11: CENSUS ENUMERATOR WITH FARMER 1930. 37
FIGURE 12: 1930 CENSUS OF LITTLE TOWNSHIP. 38
FIGURE 13: WRITING IMPLEMENTS, LATE 20TH CENTURY. 42
FIGURE 14: US MARSHALS SERVED AS THE FIRST 45
FIGURE 15: AN EARLY COPY MACHINE. 46
FIGURE 16: A CENSUS-TAKER ILLUSTRATION 1870. 48
FIGURE 17: LETTER FROM JOHN QUINCY ADAMS TO HIS FATHER IN 1777. 53
FIGURE 18: JOHN QUINCY ADAMS AS A YOUNG MAN. 53
FIGURE 19: PHOTOGRAPHER USING A NECK BRACE. 57
FIGURE 20: DAGUERREOTYPE OF WILLIAM DUDREY ABOUT 1864. 58
FIGURE 21: THIS 8x10 TINTYPE PICTURE 60
FIGURE 22: UNION SOLDIER, SITTING IN NECK BRACE 61
FIGURE 23: REVENUE STAMPS 63
FIGURE 24: WILLIAM PRETTYMAN, FRONTIER PHOTOGRAPHER. 64
FIGURE 25: A FAMILY IN THEIR DUGOUT HOME IN THE CHEROKEE STRIP ABOUT 1894. 65
FIGURE 26: CABINET CARD PHOTO 67
FIGURE 27: A RARE 1840S DAGUERREOTYPE PHOTO, UNIDENTIFIED MODEL. 68
FIGURE 28: THIS LADY IS DRESSED IN THE 1860S 69
FIGURE 29: BONNETS, BUSTLES, & DRESS STYLES FROM THE 1840S. 70
FIGURE 30: MR. AND MRS. TITUS BUFFINGTON 71
FIGURE 31: RESEARCH RECORD LOG. 75
FIGURE 32: ROYAL COAT OF ARMS 82
FIGURE 33: DESIGN YOUR OWN! 84
FIGURE 34: BINDERS FOR YOUR FAMILY GROUP SHEETS (FGS). 86
FIGURE 35: A FAMILY ALBUM FROM MINNESOTA WITH PHOTOS. 92
FIGURE 36: FINDING UNCLE LEVI. 108
FIGURE 37: FINDING A GEOCACHE. 113
FIGURE 38: FAUSSET FAMILY BURIAL GROUND, ... 117

FIGURE 39: STACKING STONES	118
FIGURE 40: A TREE EATING A TOMBSTONE IN KENTUCKY	120
FIGURE 41: BEFORE AND AFTER CLEANING.	121
FIGURE 42: FIVE TINY STONES TELL A STORY.	123
FIGURE 43: EXAMPLES OF TREE STUMP TOMBSTONES.	126
FIGURE 44: MASONIC SYMBOLS.	132
FIGURE 45: A DEATH MASK.	140
FIGURE 46: GUARD DOG IN KENTUCKY CEMETERY.	140
FIGURE 47: DEATH'S HEAD OR SOUL EFFIGY TOMBSTONES	141
FIGURE 48: THE WEEPING ANGEL OF ATHENS, OH.	143
FIGURE 49: A COUNTY CLERK'S OFFICE RECORD ROOM.	158
FIGURE 50: GUARDIANSHIP	168
FIGURE 51: MARRIAGE BOND	171
FIGURE 52: JUDGE ROY BEAN'S OFFICE IN TEXAS.	175
FIGURE 53: NEWSPAPER ANNOUNCEMENT.	178
FIGURE 54: BLAZING A TRAIL.	192
FIGURE 55: THEODORE ROOSEVELT.	206
FIGURE 56: PVT. WM DUDREY 1862	207
FIGURE 57: WM DUDREY, FT LEAVENWORTH CEMETERY., KS.	208
FIGURE 58: THE LONG-ABANDONED	212
FIGURE 59: GAR SYMBOLS.	213
FIGURE 60: GAR SYMBOLS.	213
FIGURE 61: THE AUTHOR WITH HER GREAT GRANDFATHER'S STONE.	259

About the Author:

Carolyn B. Leonard shares her passion for family history with her husband as they explore historic places, photograph interesting tombstones and rummage through old courthouse records.

Figure 61: The author with her great grandfather's stone.

As a descendant of original Low Dutch settlers of New Amsterdam, for the past fourteen years she has coordinated the biennial nationwide Dutch Cousins Gathering and overseeing projects that include preserving a two-hundred-year-old meetinghouse in Mercer County, Kentucky.

The KY Governor named her an honorary Kentucky Colonel for publicizing the sixteenth century Reformed Dutch migration from New Jersey through Pennsylvania to Kentucky. The Kentucky Sons of American Revolution awarded her a medal of honor for identifying Revolutionary War veterans and locating their graves. Research on family lines have led her to Germany, England, the Netherlands, and libraries all across the United States.

Leonard is an active member of several genealogical societies, Oklahoma Prairies DAR (Daughters of American Revolution), Daughters of 1812, the prestigious Mayflower Society, First Families of the Oklahoma Twin Territories, and historical societies in several states.

She enjoys presenting programs or teaching classes to help people find their family's place in history and can be reached through her website at www.CarolynBLeonard.com or by email to CarolynLeonard@me.com

Books by Carolyn B. Leonard, available in bookstores and from Amazon.com.

Who's Your Daddy? (2nd Edition)
A Guide to Genealogy from Start to Finish
ISBN 13: 978-1-883852-08-5 (softcover)
Daddy 13: 978-1-883852-11-5 (e-book)
Hardback ISBN 978-1-883852-19-1
Library of Congress Control Number: 2018906060
Size 6x9, 270 pages, 60 illustrations
Spine width 0.614 inches weight 0.891 lb

To Israel, With Love: (2nd Edition)
A Journey of Discovery in History,
Mystery, Travel, and Relationships ...
in full color and large print.
ISBN 13: 978-1883852-09-2 (softcover)
Israel 13: 978-883852-10-8 (e-book)
Hardback ISBN 13: 978-1883852-18-4
Library of Congress control number 2018902864
Size 8x10, 280 pages, 202 illustrations

The First Hundred Years
The US Presidents, the Federal Census,
and Current Events
that Influenced the Lives of your Ancestors 1790-1890
ISBN 13: 978-1-883852-12-2 (softcover)
Hundred 13: 978-1-883852-13-9 (e-book)
Hardback ISBN: 978-1-883852-14-6
Library of Congress control number: 2019901259
Paperback size 6x9, 340 pages, 76 illustrations
Cream paper, Georgia font size 12 text
https://amzn.to/33n82b2

Coming soon:
The Second Century
The US Presidents, the Federal Census,
and Current Events
that Influenced the Lives of your Ancestors 1900-1970
ISBN 13: 978-1-883852-15-3 (softcover)
Second Century e-book ISBN 13: 978-1-883852-16-0
Hardback ISBN 13: 978-1-883852- 17-7
Size 6x9, pages, illustrations

www.ingramcontent.com/pod-product-compliance
Lightning Source LLC
Chambersburg PA
CBHW030106240426
43661CB00001B/27